# *The* TRUTH *Within the* SILENCE

## CECELIA IBARRONDO

PAGE PUBLISHING, INC.
New York, NY

First originally published by Page Publishing, Inc. 2018

ISBN 978-1-64424-575-0 (Paperback)
ISBN 978-1-64424-576-7 (Digital)

Printed in the United States of America

To my children, my mother, and those who have experienced rough patches through the journey of life.

"Dear God, I am surrendering the heavy load that I have been carrying for a long time. Give me peace and joy and set me free from the people who have hurt me."

# FOREWORD

My life, like many others, has not been what I have expected. I have stumbled many times as I walked through my path. Pain and hardships had been so familiar in my life at such a young age that presently, it feels strange living without it.

I grew up with a large family on an island in the 1970s. My mother was born in 1928, and she carried her old ways throughout her life. I lived in a world full of secrets, jealousy, and resentment while walking under the sunny blue skies of St. Kitts. I ate my dinner made of natural resources among a household of hate and deceit and bathed in the cool, peaceful ocean all while Mom carried a heavy burden from the repercussions of giving me life. This is my story.

# CHAPTER ONE

I walked over to the shared dresser and looked into the mirror. Here I am, skinny and very short, my cheeks high and prominent on my dark face, and my gapped teeth and wide smile that I don't care for bright against my skin.

Growing up can be rough, especially as a young child with very short hair, so short and thin you could see more scalp than hair, and it doesn't help that it stuck up everywhere. "Bag of bones" is what some would refer to me as because of my thinness. My forehead, too prominent for my liking, is routinely covered with braids and that would also hide the fact that I barely had eyebrows.

I live in a seven-bedroom house overlooking the ocean in a village of a small sunny island named St. Kitts. There are two floors. The second floor is the main entrance as our home sits on an angle of what used to be a mountainous area in this part of the village. Most of the homes are angled in this manner. Our little brown-painted home was built from the ground up by Dad and a few others. He is very hardworking like my mom. Mom's hard work takes place on her farm on the mountains as well as our backyard where we have our chickens and other animals. She maintains a garden full of breadfruit trees, avocados, mangos, string beans, peanuts, bananas, teas, and more.

We are a very fortunate family; the house we live in is small for such a large family, but we manage. The girls sleep three to a bed, and the boys each have their own beds but not necessarily their own rooms. Two of my brothers were given beds outside bedrooms on the lower level, but not one of us has ever complained. We don't see anything wrong with it. I suppose that's just how we were raised. Mom raised us to respect our elders and to always help one another. We were never ashamed of what we had or didn't have. Life and living is so much more important than material things. There is always food on the table, and the house is always clean. We have always been grateful for what we have but even with all the children in the house, there is always a lot of silence.

I am the last of the fourteen siblings, three died before I was born, and one was a miscarriage. I have six brothers and four sisters. There is a twenty-year gap between myself and my eldest sibling, so when I was born, there were a few siblings who were already living on their own.

Life on the island is simple enough. Everyone knows you or knows of you, and it is really easy to get by with little money. Mom often trades her goods with her neighbors or other farmers for other things that she may need to prepare for dinner. Oftentimes, my brothers would come home with five dollars' pay for the week and buy bread and cheese and a Bryson (soda) for ten cents! Occasionally he treats himself to a brand-new pair of pants for two dollars and saves the rest of his money until the next pay week. I like to buy candy. You can buy so much for just a penny!

Moments like that make me happy. It helps me forget how much I hate being home with Dad. Things have been tough for me recently because I am starting to feel like an outcast. My brothers pick on me and Dad ignores me so sometimes I feel lonely when Mom isn't around. Being the last kid is tough since all my siblings are older. I just don't have anyone to play with. Dad is so nice to everyone but me, and I find myself wishing that I could be more like my siblings. So for now, Mom is my best friend.

I don't know why Dad doesn't seem to like me. I always make sure to say my greetings to him whenever I see him just like Mom told me to do. Whenever I say "good morning" or "good afternoon," he simply ignores me and my presence. He doesn't even look into the direction of my voice as if I don't exist. Whenever Mom needs something from him, she sends me over to talk to him, and when I address him, he yells at me. He scolds me for calling him Dad, and everyone else calls him that, so why can't I?

It really bothers me that Dad won't speak to me. I still continue to address him by his name because that is the right thing to do. I don't want to be disrespectful.

"You are too dark and ugly to be my child!" he would say, but I think he says that because most of my siblings are clear like him while some of us are dark like Mom.

Many times, I cry in the corner of my room and other times, I whine to Mom. "Why is Dad ignoring me?" I would ask.

"Nah bother wit' 'im. He a drink too much. He a mean, nasty man."

And boy do I believe her, but it still hurts me just the same. I just hated being ignored, especially by Dad. I always feel guilty as if I did something to upset him. Whenever Dad and I are in the same room, his demeanor would change. The air in the room feels heavy, my body feels warm, and the palms of my hand begin to sweat. Sometimes Dad would glare at me and twist his lips into a vicious snarl, exposing his teeth like a ravenous animal. Most days, his face would give the most incredulous look of disgust I had ever seen, and whenever I would make eye contact, I had a sinking feeling in the pit of my stomach. But whenever Mom is around, I always feel safe, and it didn't matter how Dad would look at me so long as Mom is by my side.

Mom is a very petite woman who is barely five feet tall and very strong. She has shoulder-length black hair that she wears in five braids. Four of those braids are cornrows worn to the back of her head and the fifth is always braided across her forehead from right to left. Mom says braiding her hair that way "to show her beauty." Her eyelids hang low and she has high cheekbones like me with a nose that is both flat and wide. She has a wholehearted laugh that would make her belly rise and fall in her dresses. My mom is beautiful.

Dad is the complete opposite of Mom in every way. His mother was a mean white woman from Poland. He carried her features well:

tall and skinny with a sharply pointed nose and small thin lips. Dad is fair-skinned with curly hair that he wears slicked back. He is very quiet, always serious, and he almost never smiles. He's a simple man that works to provide for us all. His daily routine consists of eating, sleeping, and waking up to do it all over again the next day. But Dad carries a very dark side, sometimes mischievous, that would arise from time to time.

Mom and Dad have a trying marriage. They seem to fight more than they do anything else. It's rare to see them smiling in the same room. Come to think of it, it's a rare sight to see them talking to one another. Dad would always fight with Mom in silence, and my brothers and I never knew what was going on, but when Dad gives Mom a certain look, we know we have to leave the room. Sometimes I will go outside and wait for her to return, and most times, she'll come back crying.

We would never hear them fight as there's never an argument. No yelling. No screaming.

Mom and Dad work really hard to keep their business to themselves as everyone on the island would. Privacy is key to our culture. A child should never get themselves involved in grown-up business, and when Mom and Dad fight, the neighbors never hear what's going on. I don't think they will ever know that there is love lacking in our household.

I know something isn't right. Why is her face always full of tears? "Mama, wa gyan?" (What's going on?) "Wa Daddy a say to you?"

No response. She never answers me whenever I ask her, but I still continue to ask anyway.

Dad comes home drunk every day. After work, he goes drinking at a nearby shack with locals. After some time, he comes home to eat the dinner Mom prepared for him. Every day at the same time, he would come home, and every day, Mom would prepare his food in a timely manner so his food would be piping hot. My siblings and I never eat at the table with him. Sometimes my brother Carnel is the only one brave enough to sit across him. It upsets Dad but not enough for either of them to get up and walk away. Some days, Dad will yell at Carnel and tell him to leave, but Carnel always remains in his seat. He's the pacifist of the family, the Rastafarian. He's the glue that keeps us all together. Whenever a fight would break out, my big brother would come to the rescue. If Dad tried to hit Mom, Carnel was always there to protect her. Some days, I wonder if Dad is afraid of Carnel, my tall, loving brother who spends his days reading, smoking, and fiddling with his guitar.

Every day, Dad would come home from work drunk and would eat his food that Mom cooked for him. He would always eat alone. I would never eat at the table with him or watch TV because I wasn't allowed to.

# CHAPTER TWO

Today had been a great day. It was a beautiful Sunday morning. The sun, hot as ever as we all had on our Sunday's best for church. Adults are carefully guiding the elders down the cobble stair of the church. I see some of my classmates running past to try to sneak a ride on the sugarcane train. There are loads of vans parked out front and drivers waiting to take the families back to their parish.

I inhaled deeply and caught the whiff of burning cane from in town. Sometimes on a windy day ash from the production site would land on the windows and our clothes. Those days could be tough, especially for me as I never wore pants, so I would have to try to shield my eyes and hold my skirt down at the same time! But not today, it was gorgeous. Mom and I carefully crossed the street making sure there were no speeding cars in sight. I looked over at Mom and could see that she was thinking intently.

Once we arrived home, Mom told me that I needed to start praying every night before bed time. She wants me to memorize most of the scriptures in the book of Psalms. She said it was mandatory, so I guess I need to get started. I don't know why she wants me to, but I won't question it. Maybe she wants to keep me protected through religion. I enjoy reading and going through the Bible because it helps me learn more words. Not many six-year-olds can read as well as I do. My new interest in reading has helped keep me distracted from Dad's mistreatment. I don't care dad ignores me, but I still love him.

With each passing moment, I grew closer and more protective of Mom as she is the only one that has showed me love. So far, she has taught me how to remain strong through my difficult times. There were days when Mom would remind us of a strict sergeant and anything she says, in our eyes, is always right. She expected us to have good posture, be well-mannered, and never talk back. We wouldn't dare mumble under our breath; otherwise, she would slap us on our mouths. Mom has very keen hearing, and it seems as if she's was always around no matter where you were.

# CHAPTER THREE

When Mom goes to the mountains to tend to a plot of farmland, she occasionally walks by my classroom to see what I am doing. She knew of my bad habit, my comfort, and my need to suck my index and middle finger. She would catch me sucking my fingers and *bam*! A slap across the face. Out of nowhere, from the side entrance, the back, and the front, every single day, she would catch me. I just wish the doors and windows of the school would stay closed from time to time.

Sucking my fingers is a comfort; it gives me a sense of security. How does she know when I'm sucking my fingers? I try changing my seat in hopes that she won't see me but that hasn't worked yet. Sometimes I would see stars in my eyes from the hard slaps, and my lips would swell. Mom doesn't seem to care. She would simply walk in, pass the teacher and say "good afternoon," then slap me in the face and walk out, leaving me stunned. Mom can be tough and there is no such thing as talking back, and she is adamant about nipping bad habits in the bud. My siblings, as I, as well as our neighbors, hold our deepest regards and respect for her as a woman and our mother.

Mom has been teaching me how to cook and wash clothes; she says these are skills she finds to be valuable in the development of a female child. Through my father and my siblings, I have been practicing these new chores. There are days when I am afraid to learn, but

I remain persistent because I want so badly for Dad to speak to me. Even with all my effort, it isn't working.

Dad throws the food that I make for him outside over the landing (porch). After enough times for that reason alone, I am convinced that he doesn't like me. Every time he throws out my plate of food that I worked so hard to prepare, I would cry and Mom would find something soothing to make me feel better.

"*Nuh* [don't] worry. He a drink too much."

It's true, Dad does drink a lot, but we all forget when he goes to watch television. After his meal, he likes to watch TV, and usually, my siblings would watch with him. Not many families have televisions in their home. My guess is that there is just so much to do around the house that people don't have time for them. I have always been curious to see what's so interesting on the TV, and every now and then, I would hide on the staircase and peer through the banister to see what was so funny. It's nice to catch a glimpse, but sometimes I can't hold in my laughter and Dad would catch me and send me out of the room. Whenever I'm caught, I end up crying out of frustration. I always have to move quickly because if I don't move fast enough, Dad will throw the nearest object at me, so it's always best to run; but I just want to watch TV like everyone else.

It hurts me knowing that I can't watch TV or be in the same room as him.

"Why Mom? Why doesn't he like me at all?"

"Don't bother with him. He's a sick man."

# CHAPTER FOUR

Mom told me to stand facing the sun to try to determine the time of day. We were held back longer than we usually worked for the day and seemed to have been running out of daylight. Mom looked worried and began to stress when I told her what time I thought it was based on my shadow. She didn't own a watch as many people didn't own them at the time.

Quickly, Mom gathered her things and told me to hurry and grab the bag of peanuts and we scurried back down the mountain. We walked through the beaten path and proceeded under the arch. We walked about two miles on the dirt road back home, and I barely kept up with Mom. She was walking so fast! Mom was in a rush to prepare dinner. We finally made it home, and Mom ran into the kitchen and began preparing our meal.

Everyone reported to dinner at the same time. We knew what time she was cooking, and no one liked eating cold food so that, among other reasons, ensured that we were all in the house eating. No conflict with Dad and the boys. They didn't want Dad to think that he was getting less food than them. Hugh would have okra and cornmeal—his special meal. He just loves cornmeal. Most of us would go outside to eat. Carol would sit by the ledge and watch the ocean. Rasta and Dad were the only people that would eat at the dinner table. He was the only brave soul to eat with him. He was the only one that was not intimidated by him. Mom would eat outside by the step.

After all the meals were done, I had to wash the dishes. Mom would try to wash dishes, but I would turn her away because I believe she works too hard. She shouldn't have to do more work after her long days in the field.

# CHAPTER FIVE

Mom has a golden apple tree in the yard. The fruit is similar to the shape of a mango but the color of a Granny Smith apple during its initial growth. When it matures and ripens, it changes from green to yellow, thus the reason why it's called a golden apple. I like to climb our golden apple tree in hopes to find the golden yellow fruit as they were the sweetest ones.

Mom went to the mountains this morning, so I have the entire day to myself, well, sort of. My brother is watching me. I walked to the back and carefully climbed the nails that resembled crucifixion spikes to the highest point of the tree. I know I'm taking a chance. The top of the tree is just so thin. I put my left leg on one of the branches and suddenly found myself falling down. I was coming down so fast I didn't have a chance to grab a limb.

My leg got caught onto one of the iron pieces, and the back of my left thigh split open. I looked down saw white meat from inside my leg it must be five inches wide and three inches deep. I didn't cry. I think I was in shock. One of my brothers took me into his room.

"Mom can't find out about this. She will know that I wasn't watching you."

We couldn't let Mom know that I was unsupervised, or we both will get beatings so we decided to hide the wound. My brother Hugh burned a needle and thread it and sewn my leg back together. I was in so much pain that I couldn't even scream, but I was hot and full of sweat. After he finished the stitchwork, he plucked a feather from one of our ducks and splashed some Bactine on my leg.

Now that my leg is stitched back together, I just need to avoid getting dressed in front of Mom. I don't know how I'm going to do it because even now as I speak, my leg is stiffening up from the pain.

# CHAPTER SIX

I have an aunt that currently lives in England. She is my mom's sister. She routinely sends boxes of clothes, food, toys, and whatever else she thinks we would enjoy. Today, I happened to get a doll! It's my first real doll. All my other dolls were handmade, but this one is just beautiful! She's porcelain with blond, curly hair and bright, blue eyes. It's rare to see dollies such as these on the island, and I am lucky enough to own one of the few!

My cousin next door called asked me to bring the doll to her house so she could see what she looks like. Before hanging up, she told me to be careful when going down the stairs. She knows how frightened I am of our staircase. It's concrete like the landing, but we don't have any railings so whenever I look down, I get a strange feeling. Sometimes I feel dizzy and other times I feel as if I'm falling over, so I take the long way to the backyard by walking through the front entrance of the house and walking down the side path.

Today, I was so excited to show off my new doll that I decided a quick walk down the concrete stairs would be okay so long as I lean against the wall of the house as I walk down. I had to be quick because Mom didn't want me to show anyone my doll in fear that someone would steal it or I simply break it. When Mom went to do chores, I took the first step down and went over. I fell over the staircase that leads to the balcony. Mom had just placed our old sewing machine by the landing (porch) to junk, and there, it was making contact with my face.

The second my face hit the sewing machine, the lower half of my nose that connects to my lip had split apart. There wasn't anything to hold that piece of flesh together. There was blood everywhere!

Mom took me to the hospital, and the doctor told me that I needed to get stitches to try to reconnect my nose and lip back together. I had so many stitches, and I kept bleeding through the bandages. He told me that eating would be difficult, but I didn't know that I wouldn't be able to eat for weeks.

Mom has been making me conky (grated coconut, grated potatoes, flour, and sugar) baked to eat. I think she meant well, but the flour and sweet potatoes just aren't soft enough to eat without having to chew a bit. She would try to smash food for me and push it to the side of my mouth so all I have to do is swallow. It's been painful, and every now and then, the wound starts bleeding.

I just wish my siblings would stop laughing at me. This is my favorite food, and I can't enjoy it anymore because now all I think about is blood, pain, embarrassment, and the taste of my salty tears. I just couldn't wait for the moment I could get these stitches removed and eat other foods.

It was the toughest three weeks of my life. I had to wait an extra week after I tried eating a normal meal and split part of my stitches open. When it was time for me to go back to the hospital to remove the stitches, I was told that we waited too late to remove the stitches and have my skin healed over the thread. Maybe it won't look so bad when I get older.

# CHAPTER SEVEN

Acceptance.

Something a young girl had to learn about very quickly. I had to come to terms with the conditions of my life—the things that couldn't be changed. I accepted it, everything she has ever said and everything he did until the day Mom made me the one solely responsible for washing Dad's oily clothes. Dad works as an engineer and every day, he comes home with dirty clothes for me to wash. After his meal, he tosses his clothes in a bucket that he had waiting for me. I think the worse feeling about washing his clothes is the moment I see the oil separating from his clothing and rising to the top of the bucket in glimmering swirls. I cry every day that I have to see those swirls.

As if things couldn't get any worse, Mom tells me that I have to go to the mountains to pick and pull peanuts. Mom has a few cows and a small patch of farmland up in the mountains. She says it's my responsibility to let the cows roam around to eat and exercise. I don't mind it so much, but the bulls have long, pointed horns that are so sharp that they intimidate me. These animals are so huge that eventually, caring for them became harder than farming. They were so aggressive and always chased after me, but no matter how far away I ran, they always knew to return back to the farm.

It would be nearing, if not one hundred degrees with the scorching sun burning my skin. Some days it's difficult to breathe from the high altitude and the humidity; it always feels a thousand times hotter than what it is. It's a tough job to manage, but I do it. I do it for Mom. I just don't understand why I am the only one doing it. A little break here and there would be nice, especially since I have to wash his clothes.

I wash Dad's clothes every day, Monday to Sunday, and so far, there hasn't been a day when I finished before the sun set. Mom would hand me the wooden brush and washboard for his clothes along with two pails: one for washing and one for rinsing. I hate it so much. I thought things would have gotten easier, but I still cry as I scrub. Meanwhile, all my siblings are going out with their friends or sleeping as I'm slaving over his clothes.

These new chores are becoming a routine for me; Mom doesn't have to tell me when to wash Dad's clothes anymore. Now, he has them outside waiting for me each and every day.

Sometimes I look up and see Dad watching me cry as I wash his oily clothes with a smile on his face. He enjoys it—my misery.

# CHAPTER EIGHT

I finished my chores for the day and now, I'm going to relax bit in the backyard. I'm not sure what game I'm going to play today, perhaps a British queen, or an adventurer exploring the jungle. This afternoon is going to be great! Mom should be home soon so I won't be alone for long.

"Hey, Charmane, do you want to play?" said a mysterious voice whispered through a hole in the fence.

I walked over to the hole to see who it was. It was a young woman. I've seen her around a few times before, but I've never actually spoken to her, so I told her no.

She wants me and my cousin that lives next door to go to the beach with her. She left abruptly and came back with my cousin. She told me it was okay for the three of us to hang out now that we were all together.

"There's nothing to be afraid of. Just come with me. Let's take a walk on the beach."

I looked over at my cousin, and she seemed okay with the idea, so I followed the two of them down the dangerous path toward the beach. It's a hot day today. The weatherman said the high would be 101 degrees, and I can feel it! While we were walking toward the beach, I started to worry. I wonder if Mom would be okay with us going out with this woman, especially since I didn't tell her or anyone else where I was going. All of a sudden, my train of thought was distracted by the loud cracking sound of a whip.

This mysterious young woman pulled three vines off the tree and braided it into a whip as we took our trek down the path. *She tricked us!* Immediately I knew we were in danger. This woman didn't want to play with us; she wanted to kidnap us, but why?

When we reached the beach, my cousin and I began to cry for help.

She tricked us into going and she kidnapped us and brought us to the beach in a 101-degree weather. She told us to kneel on the scorching sand, and we did. She continued to whip us as our knees blackened from the heat. She then forced us to eat baracada, a poisonous fruit that grows on the trees near the beach. Its sole purpose is to help maintain the shape of the beach to prevent eroding.

I looked over at my cousin, and I whispered to her, "Don't swallow, just try to pretend."

It was hard to see past the large drops of tears, but I knew she was scared. Are we going to die right here on this beach? All of a sudden, I saw Mom running toward us with a big stick in her hand.

Her face was full of sweat as she came forward with a big stick in her hand. We still had the fruit in our mouths, shocked as Mom chased the girl; but Mom couldn't keep up with her and immediately turned toward us and chased us with the same stick back home. We got up so fast and didn't look back. All you could see was the sand flying up behind us because we were running so fast.

Mom took us straight to the hospital and upon our release, my cousin and I were no longer allowed to speak to one another again. Mom told me later that the mysterious girl who kidnapped us was Hugh's ex-girlfriend. She wanted to get back at him for breaking her heart. The only way she knew was through family. She wanted to kill us to hurt him.

Mom said she immediately realized that we were missing when she came home from the mountains. One of our neighbors saw us walking to the beach with that young woman and that's when Mom knew we were in trouble. Mom and I have an agreement that I could never leave the house unless given permission.

# CHAPTER NINE

Well, nothing mattered to me anymore. I don't have my father's love or attention, and I'm starting to feel very lonely. Doing my chores seems to be the other thing that I can look forward to. It's the only thing that remains consistent in my life.

Mom thinks it's best to take me to the mountains more often, especially on the weekends just so Dad won't be left alone to mistreat me while she's away. These trips are going to become a part of my routine, I just know it. I started praying harder after she gave me the devastating news because I hate the mountains; I hate getting up to meet her near her plot of land at 5:00 a.m. I know once I get there, we won't come back home until after the sun goes down. Now, not only do I have to tend to the cows and help pick peanuts; I have to pull yams, pumpkins, watermelon, peas, and peppers for Mom to sell.

Mom says the best way to carry the bag of goods is by putting it on my head. It's better than holding them in my hand, as my arms get tired so quickly, but sometimes I would slip down the hill with the bags of potatoes on my head. It's so heavy, especially since I can carry more on my head, but my neck would twist with pain if I turned my head too quickly.

Sometimes Mom and I would make coal for her to sell and use for cooking. I started helping her picking and layering the kasha branches because she would occasionally get hit with sparks of hot debris. The kasha branches are layered with hay before setting them ablaze. Once the fire is set, we then cover the pit with dirt and wait for the pit to sink then carefully collect the coals and place them in a bag to sell.

One day after collecting the coal, Mom and I began our journey back home. She was singing a hymn, and I was just listening to her pretending I was somewhere else when suddenly the bag of coal caught on fire on top of my head! I dropped the bag and screamed. Mom stopped and looked around to see what was wrong. She had the look of annoyance as if I was disturbing her. She looked as if she was about to hit me until she saw the smoldering bag on the ground.

She immediately grabbed dirt and threw it onto the bag to out the fire.

Tears started to fall from my face as I continued to walk a few steps behind Mom. I didn't want Mom to know that I was injured. I wanted to be tough like her. When we finally made it home, Dad was standing on the balcony watching Mom with such a cold look in his eyes. I don't know what the look was for, but I was certain he was upset with her for something; but at the same time, I knew I had clothes to wash, so I went straight to the buckets where he left his clothes to soak. I was so tired and worn-out from such a long distance walk in the mountains. It was an hour long walk, and I still had more work to do.

Dad still isn't talking to me. It's been years and I still haven't been able to hold a conversation with him. The only time words escape his mouth is to send me out of the room he was in or to my mother. He's becoming increasingly silent with each passing year, and he's drinking more and more.

Dad's an alcoholic now, and I don't think he talks to Mom anymore. The house has grown silent, and my siblings are happy Mom and Dad aren't fighting as much, but unfortunately, it seems as if they are blind to the issues they're having.

# CHAPTER TEN

I've always had a fascination about flying, so I've spent a lot of my free time thinking about what it must feel like, especially on a breezy day. I like to believe that I'm an angel with wings soaring down over all the houses, trees, and the oceans. Whenever I think this way, I usually end up in a deep trance.

I wonder, *What would life be like if I had wings, if I were able to be able to fly?* I asked my brother Melvin what he thought about flying, if he thought it was possible for humans to do so even just for a second.

"Jump out di window gyal and see wuh 'appen." So I did.

I jumped from the second-floor window near the balcony, and as I was going down, I clapped my hands harder and harder! I could feel the breeze on my face and through my fingers, but once I realized I wasn't flying, I went down fast and *hard*! The wind was knocked out of me, and I could not move. I couldn't even call for help. I could barely breathe, but I did hear the quick pitter-patter of my brothers feet as they smacked against the tiles of our home going through the kitchen, the dining room, and living room, straight out of the door.

My brother ran away and failed to tell anyone what I did. He didn't look to see if I was standing or sitting or if I was even alive! I just laid there until Mom went to the window to toss a pot of water from the very window that I jumped out from. She looked over and saw me. All I could hear Mom saying was, "Lord, help me. Me last pickney [child]."

Mom picked me up and took me to the hospital again, and this time, I had a hole in my head. The nurses stuffed the hole with cotton balls and sewed me back up. I think they forgot to remove the cotton.

# CHAPTER ELEVEN

It's the weekend—the start of another trip to the mountains. The only difference is that I have questions for Mom that I need answers to. Since Mom thinks it's disrespectful for a child to ask an adult questions, I have to prepare for whatever comes next.

Mom says the lighter skinned children aren't allowed to go to the mountains because she didn't want them to get dark. She believes that beauty is in lighter skin, but three of my siblings are dark skinned like me, and yet they don't have to go either.

"Why am I the only person going to the mountains?"

I have no other choice it seems. I need school clothes and books, so I have to go. I don't think it would be so bad if I could go to other places besides school and church.

There are so many people that I consider to be strangers that actually like me and want to be my friend. I know that I'm growing up and that means that I have a little more freedom than I had before, but I still feel left out since I don't have any friends. It's just me and her.

I'm eight years old, and now, I'm learning more about myself. I have a new hobby now. I like to braid hair. I didn't know how skilled I was at this until the neighborhood kids started coming around.

I don't mind braiding the kids' hair that live in the village. I think that it helps build their self-esteem when they look good. I know a lot of the children in the poor area don't have nice clothes, so at least they can go to school and look decent.

I'm becoming really good at this skill and even adults are coming around to ask me to braid their hair, but whenever I'm aware that they're looking for me I tend to hide. It's not that I don't want to do their hair, it's just that I don't know how to socialize with them. I'm really shy and I spend so much time with Mom that I usually get a little nervous around unfamiliar people.

It's rare to see neighborhood kids around my age. Mom's friends that have children are practically adults like my brothers and sisters. I feel so odd. I just want to feel normal, and the only time that I do is when I'm braiding hair. It's the only time that I feel wanted and included.

While Mom was away selling peanuts, I invited one of the kids over to wash and braid their hair. I'm usually very strategic about how I get these kids to the backyard. I try to avoid being seen because I don't know how Mom would feel about these kids being around our home. But this particular day, everything seemed just fine, so I started washing this little girl's hair under the pipe when Mom came home. She arrived much earlier than I had expected. It turns out, she wasn't selling those peanuts but rather making a trade with someone in the area. She ran the little girl from off out property and told me that she didn't want the neighborhood kids around.

"Me know ya mean well buhya cyant 'ave dis chil'ren in me home. Yuh nah know a way dey lookin' for." (I can't have the children in her home. I know you mean well, but they might want something.)

So she suggested that if I'm going to continue, I should consider helping family instead. I agreed because I didn't want to be lonely.

# CHAPTER TWELVE

Well, here comes Dad.

Had to get out of his way because I'm afraid of him. His presence is scary.

He passed me straight, without a word, like I was invisible to him.

I'm becoming hard, my heart is turning to stone, and I've learned how to cry on the inside because of the pain I feel. I have to numb myself from these experiences in order to continue on. Dad is always running the grandkids out the house, and he's still sending me outside to Mom.

Some days it's just so he wouldn't see my face, and other times, it's to "help her fight." I just don't understand. Why is he fighting Mom, and why is it my job to help her? And that smell of alcohol, I want to ask him, why? so badly, but I'm so afraid of him, and I'm tired of being sent away when I want to talk to him.

His silence is so scary.

As the days go by, I begin to think, *I am tired of cleaning, washing, and cooking*. These chores keep me busy until nearly 10:00 p.m. every night. I pray to God asking, "Why me? What have I done?" and once I've finished my prayer, I'd fall asleep waiting for the answer. I share Mom's bed because I feel safe there with her, and that's where I slept until I was about thirteen years old.

# CHAPTER THIRTEEN

It's a new year, and nothing seemed to have changed. Mom is still farming and selling goods; I'm still doing my household chores. Maybe I've gotten better at cooking, I guess. But Dad is still just as distant as I could remember.

I just finished praying and was getting ready for bed. Mom was already in bed, so I was trying to be careful not to wake her. I pulled the sheets over and got into bed, careful to hide my hand as I sucked my fingers. As I was lying in bed, I looked over to my right and saw a figure standing in the doorway. I was so afraid, and I didn't know what to do. I was too afraid to scream so I just kept staring. It was a man, he was very tall, almost too big to walk through the doorway, and was wearing all white. He looked at me with his hands crossed over his chest like a mummy, and he gave me a faint smile. He didn't look scary, but friendly or rather, inviting.

I tried to wake Mom up. I called for her and shook her, but she didn't budge. This was the first and only time that I was unable to wake my mother up, and she is a light sleeper. So here I was, left alone with this figure standing there looking at me. I was frightened and mystified at the same time. It seemed like everything was at a standstill besides myself and this man in white. I couldn't hear the ocean, the crickets, or the clock. Was this God? Have I died? Am I going to heaven?

There's no way I'm looking at God. I didn't do anything to hurt myself. I can't be dying. Suddenly, he flared his wings that were hiding behind his back and long, white gown.

Everything around him seemed to be brighter. He was surrounded by white light, almost too bright for my own eyes to see. It seemed as if we were connected, as if things were familiar, and I felt so safe. We shared that connection for maybe ten seconds, but it felt like an eternity.

I grabbed my sheet and placed it over my head. I took a deep breath and squeezed my eyes shut. I peeked one eye over from under the covers, and he was still there! When I was brave enough to remove those sheets from my face completely, he was gone.

He was gone, Mom woke up, the clock started ticking, and the ocean waves roared and splashed against the rocks. If I didn't believe in God, angels, and heaven before, this would have been a shocker, but this experience has strengthened my faith. I know that there is something or someone who is more powerful than us humans here on earth. There is something greater than us out there.

I believe this experience was a significant moment in my life. My faith had grown as well as my strength. I was determined to be in a better situation. I want to be happy, and I've made the decision that I would pray harder and ask God to please send an angel to rescue me from this painful house of sorrow.

# CHAPTER FOURTEEN

I'm getting older, and I think that Mom is starting to feel bad or at least notice my need for friendships outside her own. There's a family that lives down the alley way not far from our house; they have a set of twins. Mom finally gave me permission to play with them. They used to come around and ask Mom all the time if I could come out and play.

The only thing is I can only play with them at night, so just after 11:00 p.m. we meet at the outside light post. Sometimes I feel like she's trying to hide me, or at least prevent the neighbors from seeing me. Either way, I'm happy to finally get out and make some friends. It's actually pretty fun trying to play games within the lighted area. They're the only kids that I'm allowed to play with at night. There's another kid in the neighborhood that I have befriended, a boy.

I know Mom wouldn't like that too much if she found out, but he's a cool kid. He's creative like me, and every time we hang out, we create something interesting! He knew that I made my own dolls out of old clothes and pillow stuffing. One day, we were walking around and my flip-flop broke! Leroy didn't have any shoes, so he was already barefoot. It was too hot for me to walk barefoot, so I needed a solution, but I didn't have another pair of shoes.

"Chamee, we have an idea. Let's make some shoes."

We walked over the hill and slid down. He passed me four pieces of slate, and he picked up an old tire. We trekked back up the hill and sat under the shade. Leroy tried to attach rubber bands to the wood in an attempt to make slippers, but the rubber bands didn't hold. So Leroy used the rubber from the tire to make our shoes. The shoes lasted for some time especially since we couldn't afford to buy shoes. No more walking on that hot pavement, which sometimes feels like walking on a hot steam table.

# CHAPTER FIFTEEN

It was recess, and I was standing beside the Tamarind tree. Some of the tamarinds were green, but the brown ones, my favorite, were dangling off those thick branches. I really wanted a snack, so I picked up a few rocks and began throwing them at the tree. Normally, I would just climb to pick my favorite tamarinds, but this tree was just too tall to climb.

I reached down to pick up my sweet, delicious treat, and when I looked over, I saw the shoes belonging to a very familiar friend. One of the twins was standing off into the corner as if she was waiting for me. My favorite twin reached out for my tamarinds right in front of my face! Boy, was I upset, so I asked her, Why? Her cousin came up behind her and told her that she didn't have to explain why and to hit me with a rock.

After school, the other twin came up to me and hit me with her ruler! I was furious! I snatched her ruler and combined it with my own and hit *both* of them with it. I dragged them both, one under each arm along the dirt road. They freed themselves from me and ran home to their mother.

The twins and their mother came to my house shortly after I arrived and started arguing with my mom! When they left, Mom beat me with wooden spoon because I "got too close" to them. She didn't want me to be too close because she believes it's safer to have friends at arm's length. After I told her my side of the story she told me that I should fight them for a second time. The thing is I just didn't want to. They were already afraid of me, so I didn't see the need to.

It seems to me that some of my classmates try to take advantage of me because I'm quiet, and because of all the times that Mom have walked in on my sucking my fingers in class.

# CHAPTER SIXTEEN

One day, Dad came home and my work was finished. All his clothes were washed. I decided to take a nap on Mom's bed. Suddenly, I woke up to find myself rolling down the fourteen steps to the lower level while still on the mattress. Dad picked me up with the mattress and threw me down the stairs from the second to the first floor. I cried over and over again and when I looked up, all I could see was Dad laughing. All I wanted was sleep from the hard day's work. Mom ran in after hearing my cries. She hopped over me and ran up the stairs after my father with a long stick and wailed, "Lawd, mi last child!"

I prayed hard that night for someone to come and rescue me.

# CHAPTER SEVENTEEN

Sugarcane was a major crop on the island and there was a train that would pass through the towns collecting crop to produce sugar and other things. It was common for kids after school and church to try to catch the train or try to get a little treat. The horn would blow when the train was full of sugarcane.

We would choose a buddy to put their head toward the ground to listen to the tracks. The vibration of the tracks determined how close the train was. The daring kids would run across the street along the train, and we would pick the canes that were sticking out from the pile. You had to look ahead of you to select the cane you wanted and you had to be fast and swift. If you went too slow, the train would drag you.

I wanted the biggest sugarcane I could grab to be tough and cool like the boys, but when I grabbed the largest one, the train pulled me forward, knocking me into the bushes and hitting a tree. You have to run fast. If you can't, don't even think about attempting this, but I really wanted to prove how tough I was and pushed the boy away that tried to help me.

# CHAPTER EIGHTEEN

Just when you thought things were getting better, Mom and Dad started silent fighting again. It was at late evening when Mom started a fire outside. She usually cooks outside to preserve what gas we had, and she says that the food tastes better when cooked outside. To make the fire, she piled together some twigs and surrounded the mound with three to four large rocks and used a match to set it all ablaze.

Mom put on the biggest pot of water on the fire to boil, and she made me sit beside it.

There's no way to avoid all the heat and the blazing smoke that went through my nose and eyes, which turned as red as the fire's flames, so I just had to sit. Looking toward the lower level entrance, I could see Dad was peeking through the top half of the stable door. He had slapped Mom earlier that day. I didn't know what Mom planned on cooking with the second pot, but just as I was about to ask her, she threw the pot of boiling hot water through the door where Dad was standing. I never saw anything like that in my life before. I was so shocked and so surprised and I know Dad was too!

The only thing I heard from Dad was "You missed me!" then he locked us both out of the house from the inside and closed all but one window. That was our only way to get inside, so Mom had me walk through her garden to a crawl in a space and go through the window from the lower level. It was such a shocking experience.

I couldn't cry for him, but I was sad for him. A week passed before I had the courage to ask Mom, "Where's Dad?" She said she didn't know, "Maybe he's drunk." That was her answer.

Mom grew worried for Dad. She continued to cook his food as he wouldn't eat from me, and yet, his food sat on the table untouched every day. Mom decided to go outside and peek through the window where Dad slept as they both had their own bedrooms. It wasn't until that very moment that I saw Mom's frantic look as she ran to get Dash. He was Dad's favorite son because he was tall and fair-skinned and shared a close resemblance to him, but not just physically; Dash himself suffered from a drinking problem as well.

When Dash entered the room, he discovered that Dad had first degree burns on his chest. The shirt he wore the day Mom attacked him was stuck to his chest, and his wound was infected. Dad had been in his room for at least a week, in pain from the scalding hot water. It appeared he couldn't take a shower, and the smell of his flesh from the infection on his body had filled the entire room. He lost significant weight from all those days of not eating, and Dash decided he would to take him to the hospital for treatment.

He came back with some kind of purple medicine rubbed all over his chest. Dad was furious with Dash because he took him to the hospital. He didn't want to go. He thought he'd heal on his own, and he didn't want people to know what his wife did to him. While he was there, Dad found out something serious about his health that he didn't want anyone to know about, not even Mom. The pain in my heart grew deeper because he was literally scarred for life, and he still didn't look at me, so I knew I couldn't ask him if he was okay.

I was dying for Dad's attention, but I didn't want to be there anymore. I couldn't handle the rejection. Dad got better in a couple of weeks and became angrier as he grew stronger, and he went back to his old ways again.

# CHAPTER NINETEEN

Mom and I were sitting in the front of the yard picking peanuts to sell when, all of a sudden, we heard the crackling sound of pebbles falling from the rooftop. We both got up to investigate the sound and saw Dad standing on the roof with a slingshot in his hand. It was made from a tree branch and two large rubber bands—something he appeared to have made himself.

Dad took that very slingshot and aimed it at the two of us. Tears rolled down my cheeks as he hit me with each shot. I screamed out loud not because of the pain, but out of frustration because I just don't understand why Dad hates me and Mom so much.

"Why, Mom? Why does he do these terrible things to us?"

Dad insisted that both Mom and I leave the village and so we did and I was happy to leave. I didn't care. We rented a house in the next village over called Challengers, and Mom took the two youngest children, myself, and my brother Mal.

I was so happy. The first night there couldn't shake this horrible feeling I had. Dad wasn't finished with us. When it became dark that night, both Mom and I were sitting outside picking peanuts while my brother was inside. It was about 11:00 p.m., and we were still trying to pack up the peanuts. It was then that I had this feeling just come over me that made me believe that Dad was coming for us. I warned Mom and she hit me, telling me to stop. "He doesn't know where we are staying—" But Dad showed up before she finished her sentence.

Dad had a big butcher knife and poked it into her side. He grabbed her by the arm and told her to walk up the stairs toward the balcony. I screamed so hard, I pleaded with him, and begged for her mercy. I was worried I would lose her. She was all I had. I tried to help her the best I could and that's when my brother Mal came running up the stairs. Dad had Mom on the top of the balcony preparing to throw her over. I screamed for help. Dad was so strong.

My brother Mal got the biggest rock he could find as I tried to hold Mom to stop her from falling over. Mal hit Dad over the head so he could let her go and it worked! We got the police to come, and they took him back to the house. During the next couple of days, we heard news from one of the oldest siblings that Dad wasn't doing too well and he wanted his wife.

Well, Mom had the duty of being a wife. She had been married to him since the age of eighteen, and she wanted to fulfill her duties. We had to move back in with him, and she brought him back to health.

# CHAPTER TWENTY

D ad was more silent than ever, and I could no longer attempt to speak to him. Mom would push me to say hello to Dad, but I couldn't. I was choking on my own words. There was so much agony in my soul. I just wanted Dad to accept me. *"Just talk to your child!"* I cried because he wouldn't even look at me. I felt so ashamed and unwanted.

I was a sad little girl.

We stayed with Dad and never went back to the new home that was in Challengers. I turned to religion; it was my only hope. I turned to my Bible and prayed more and more. I prayed for someone to take me away from this pain.

# CHAPTER TWENTY-ONE

One day, Mom sent me to feed the pigs around the corner from the house. I had to gather all the unwanted leftover food from home and a few neighbors and carried the bucket of smelly, spoiled food on my head. My second-oldest brother, Hugh, was a carpenter, and he was fixing a tourist's guesthouse at that time. I was walking toward the guest house pretending I was someone else in another world who had an English accent. As I was talking to myself, someone answered back at me. It was my angel. She was a red-haired woman with freckles, and she was the tourist staying in that very guesthouse. She had heard me talking outside her window.

She invited me inside and laughed the entire time because she had been watching me talk to myself and thought it was funny. From that moment on, we became very close. My angel.

Every day, I found myself going back to visit her when I needed to feed the pigs. We only lived four houses away from each other. Vern became my healer, a second Mom to me, and I was no longer alone.

She had a beehive in her backyard. My brother used to come and smoke the bees out and squeeze the honey out from the trays in which she kept the honeycombs. He would wear a bee suit, the younger bees sometimes did not leave the honeycombs and he would eat the honeycombs. He would offer the combs to me to suck out the juices but there would be small bee larva inside which deterred me from eating it. After the trays were cleaned, he would place them back into the bee house and the bees would come back swarming. He would remove the queen bee so the workers would follow. He would check every six months for produced honey.

After about two weeks, she asked Mom if I could live with her, and I begged Mom, "Please! Dad is treating me so cold," and I told her that I would continue to wash Dad's clothes and she said okay. That moment brought joy to my heart, and I hugged Mom, but I also feared for her safety. Mom had the biggest smile on her face because she knew that I was still close—only four houses away.

# CHAPTER TWENTY-TWO

One day, I had the courage to ask Mom, "Why are my brothers and sisters lighter than me?" They had pointed noses yet my nose was flat. Mom used to pinch my nose daily and told me that my nose was flat from sucking my thumb as a baby. She said that as I sucked my thumb, I would press my index finger across my nose, causing it to flatten. Either way, I couldn't shake the feeling that I did not belong there. I didn't look anything like my siblings and I certainly did not act like them, but I let it go.

I was happy that my angel, Vern, accepted me and loved me as her own child. We did everything together as a mother and daughter would: going to church, the beaches along the shore, washing, hiking, and traveling on the ferryboat to the different islands meeting her friends. Vern was a woman of the Peace Corps. She would go the hospital on the island and visit the sick as well as children with disabilities.

One day, she brought home a nine-year-old boy from her visit. His name was Leslie. His mother had abandoned him because he was physically disabled. I became his protector because I, myself, was unwanted so I could easily relate to him. There was beauty in his smile, and you could see his personality shine through it. The smile he had would light up the whole room, and you couldn't do anything but love him more. He had perfect teeth and the deepest dimples.

Leslie couldn't walk or talk, but Vern taught us both sign language so we could communicate with each other.

Vern decided she wanted to adopt him as her own and take him back with her to the States. I thought that was a wonderful gift to give Leslie for his previous life experiences. He deserved it. Looking back, I will never forget Vern's kindness and the hard work she put in for those sick kids.

I used to help Vern care for Leslie when she had to go out. I learned how to make underwear for Leslie out of Vern's panties because his older brother would visit him and steal all his things. Leslie laughed so hard, but he didn't seem to care. He knew that he was loved by both her and I. I felt so loved and at home with Vern until it was time for her to go back to her hometown, Kansas City.

The initial shock rushed through my heart, "*No!* I just found you!" but I kept it in knowing that she would come back to me. The most glorious thing that happened after living with her for three years: I was happy, I learned how to stay humble and to always give even if it was the last thing I had, and most importantly, I learned how to love.

It was time for Vern to go back to the States. Vern surprised me when she asked to speak to Mom. I didn't know why she wanted to talk to her. I found out later that she wanted me to take a visit with her to the United States for vacation. My eyes grew big and teary with joy. Now was the moment to escape that painful house.

My intention was to never return to St. Kitts. Dad didn't even know that I was living up the street with Vern and never asked for me. I hoped leaving would permanently erase the nightmare; I wished for Vern to adopt me along with Leslie, her soon-to-be-adopted son.

Vern finally got the okay from Mom to take me away, and Vern received visas for both Leslie and I to go to the States. I had a green suitcase (like briefcase), and it carried six panties, one bra, four church dresses, two pant suits, one green and one black, and two pairs of shoes.

Now, we were on our way to the airport. I said my goodbyes and told Mom, "I am not coming back." I was about thirteen now, leaving Mom for the first time in my life, thousands of miles away; away from the pain and the agony. Landing in Miami, next stop Kansas City!

# CHAPTER TWENTY-THREE

I was overjoyed with all these emotions to be there with my second mom. Once we were in Miami, we heard my name over the intercom. I needed to report to a gate for a connection to New York. We looked at each other with horror, as if we had seen a ghost. Vern asked me, "What's going on?" I didn't know. So she put Leslie on her hip, and she guided me to the gate to find out what was going on.

I was so upset and afraid. I found out that my oldest sister, whom I never met, bought a ticket for me to go with her instead. Vern didn't take the news too well. She broke down and Leslie's face changed almost immediately. We were all filled with disappointment. Just watching the tears rolling down his eyes sent a stabbing pain to my heart. *We were a family!* And we were being ripped apart. I cried when the agent told us my sister sent the ticket. We were pulled apart from each other's arms. I wouldn't let go.

I couldn't let go because she was my angel. In that very moment, my spirit had died knowing my angel was being taken away from me. I will never forget the pain she carried in her voice when she spoke. Why would they do that to her?

She kissed me and called me kiddo. It was her favorite name for me.

I hated them for what they did. I never grew up with them. They were strangers to me, and I was leaving my angel to be with them. I had no idea what to expect.

# CHAPTER TWENTY-FOUR

I hated my family for taking away my happiness. I felt that miserable pain over again, but I kept my faith. I wanted to go back home to be with my real mom. On my way to my gate, I ran into one of my brother's friends. He told me he was on the flight to Miami with me, but he didn't have a chance to speak to me. He wanted to know where I was headed, so I told him. I told everything, and he sat with me at the gate until my departure time.

My oldest sister Cynthia met me at the airport in New York. She was a stern woman. Her face was stolid and was tall with broad shoulders. Cynthia was dark, but not as dark as me with long jet-black hair and deep-brown eyes. I didn't have a good feeling about her, and before long, I would know all I needed to know about her.

When I got into the car, I sank into my seat and tried to hide. I never saw snow before, and it was such an amazing sight—the way it was dropping from the sky. I was scared because I thought that God was ending the world with the large snowflakes dropping, and the tall buildings that seemed as if they were closing in on me. I came in December and stayed with her until the end of January. Cynthia lived on top of a mountain. Her home was surrounded by large trees and the area was very quiet. There weren't any stores nearby as she was away from the city. It snowed heavily. You needed high boots and sleighs to go down the hill.

Cynthia had great kids. The oldest one was an artist who liked to collect Cabbage Patch Kids dolls, and the second was a clown, he enjoyed making others laughed and would occasionally dress up in Cynthia's clothes.

While I was living with her, I was mistreated and I wasn't allowed to eat certain foods in her refrigerator. She had three sons at that time, and they were her pride and joy. The food she kept in that refrigerator was solely for them. I didn't let that bother me because my main concern was to leave. I wanted to find my way back to the island as soon as possible, so I placed a collect call as soon as I learned how to do so. I wanted a ticket home.

Mom told me not to come home because Dad would mistreat me again. She said it was best for me to stay in the United States with my sister, and I felt confused, lost once again. Why wouldn't she save me?

I ended up living with my sister in New York for about two months. After living with her for a while, I realized that I had seen her once before. Cynthia had been a police officer on the island, but she wasn't living in the house by the time I was born. She didn't visit Mom except for this one time. She came to the house with a baby, and she asked Mom to care for it for her. When she left the baby boy at the house she never came back for him.

While I was in New York, I found out I had another sister living in New Jersey. She was the second oldest by the name of Pat. Both Cynthia and Pat fought over me because they each needed a sitter for their children. Pat told Cynthia she paid for the ticket and had less kids, so I should stay with her. I felt like garbage being tossed around, unwanted by my own family whom I never met. No one cared about me and my wants and needs. I was just a tool they used and abused.

# CHAPTER TWENTY-FIVE

Cynthia sent me to New Jersey with Pat and her two children, Rosalind and Victor. The second I laid eyes on Pat, I thought of one of my other sibling on the island that I grew up with. There was a striking resemblance between her and Pat, and I felt some relief. Somehow, I connected the two of them and assumed that they would share similar personalities, especially since they could pass for twins.

Rosalind was fearless, she was an athlete and didn't shy away from what boys did. She was soft-spoken and didn't like to comb her hair initially. She was obedient unlike Victor who thought he was a big man. He would dress in suits to impress my friends. He didn't go to school often, played hooky, he liked to play with his shoelaces in school, and playing pretend saying he was in space. The mistreatment from her started almost immediately. My body grew numb. The pain became all too much, but I forced myself to be happy as this situation seemed to be better than the last. I told myself that I had to do it for the kids because I never wanted them to share the experiences that I had in my life. I kept all the painful memories I had away from my siblings because they didn't seem to care about me, telling them would make no difference.

Pat enrolled me into school right away. I was happy to be back in school. It was hard for people to understand me at first, so I was always afraid to read in class. The kids would laugh at my accent and whispered about the way I spoke. I would pretend to lose my voice and pretend I had a cold, but I always did well.

I couldn't pretend any longer because my teachers said that if I didn't cooperate, I would fail my classes. It took two years to finally speak up with or without an accent. High school kids would say that I was dumb or I couldn't read because I wouldn't speak in class. I was so shy, and I didn't look anyone in their eyes. I felt ugly, and I was laughed at practically every day, especially in gym. I had a very low self-esteem.

I would bring in a note saying that I was sick and couldn't exercise until the gym teacher said I would fail and not be able to graduate. I came into gym every day from that point on. I became interested in biology, and I received a plaque for career awareness.

Some week had passed before Pat had threw me out of her house. She knew that I was in a country, let alone a different state. Everything was so unfamiliar and scary. I didn't know anyone. She kicked me out because I asked her children about Pat's friend. I wanted to know why they addressed this woman as their aunt who was not related to them. I wasn't sure if they were related in some way or if this was an American custom that I was not familiar with.

As a result, Pat yelled at me and tore the only bra I owned at the time then threw me out the house. It was cold that day, and my body couldn't take the chill. I was still trying to adjust to the seasons because I was only familiar with the one you got from an ocean breeze. I had to put my mind somewhere else just so I wouldn't feel that chill going through my body up to my brain.

Later that day, Pat finally told me to come back in the house because the kids begged for me not to leave, but I didn't want to be there any longer. I didn't feel safe. There was no security in that household, and I quickly learned how unpredictable and rash my sister could be.

# CHAPTER TWENTY-SIX

Well, it didn't take long for Pat to have her boyfriend move in after meeting him a couple of weeks before at a bus stop. He told her that his apartment had burned down, which I believed was a lie. He lived with us for a very long time in a one-and-a-half-bedroom apartment on Summit Avenue in East Orange. The three of us, Rosalind, Victor, and myself were supposed to sleep in one room with only a single bed.

Victor chose to sleep in the living room on the floor for a while. It really hurt me to see him on the floor. I was bitter because what little happiness they had was taken away from them. I had to protect the both of them, Victor and Rosalind, from this ex-Marine guy because something didn't sit right with me and my intuition was strong.

One day, I left school early due to a toothache. Pat didn't know I was home, and I overheard her boyfriend saying I was too black to be her sister and in return, I heard my sister respond and say that I didn't belong to her father. When I heard her say that I ran out of my shared room and cried, "Who is my father then?"

I was older now, about sixteen, and I was yelling at Pat. I was so enraged that my sister would dare to say such a thing. How could that be true? Mom would hear about this! I called Mom collect and asked her, "Who is my father?" She asked me where I got that idea from, and I told her Pat, her favorite daughter who she praised so much had said so.

Mom always knew the right words to say to me to calm me down. She told me, "Not to worry. I don't know why she said such a mean thing, but I will talk to her about it," and just like that, the conversation ended.

I don't know what Mom said to Pat, but I never heard her say anything like that about me or Dad again. Mom told her that she had to take care of me and gave her legal guardianship; at the same time, I was pleading to go back home. Mom told me I wasn't allowed to come back home, and I cried for weeks because I thought I did something wrong.

# CHAPTER TWENTY-SEVEN

Months went by and things got worse. My sister's boyfriend grew to hate me because I was so protective of her children. I couldn't feel pain anymore, and I learned a valuable tool—to remain silent. I learned how to push all that pain away deep down behind my heart and never let it get in the way.

On a Sunday afternoon, my sister Pat decided to bake her favorite pies for the church: pecan, apple, cherry, and blueberry (which I was not fond of). Pat always went to church at least twice a day. On this particular Sunday, Pat's boyfriend was more abusive toward her than usual. He told her that he was hungry and to serve him dinner before she went to church.

Just looking at the fear in her eyes worried me. I had to be the one to stand up for her because I was afraid for her. The evil in him reminded me of Dad. Pat told him "After church," and he went into the kitchen and flipped the stove upside down with the church pies. The anger grew within me, but I went to check on the kids. I wanted him to leave.

I told the kids that Mom and Dad used to fight every day, similar to what we were hearing at the time. I had to protect my family. I told him to leave, he put his hands up to hit me, and the first thing I grabbed in sight was a kitchen knife.

My sister defended him and pushed me outside and locked the door. I was left standing in the cold snow without shoes and a coat.

I had no more tears left. I just wanted to get inside, away from the unfamiliar cold that I was feeling. I became angrier because I didn't know what he would do to the kids.

Finally, Rosalind opened the door for me, and I decided to go to the police station and file a complaint. The kitchen walls were an array of different colors from the pies and I figured that was the best time to get the police to come into the house.

It took about forty minutes to walk to the police station and back and by the time the officers came, Pat had cleaned everything from the walls and hid him outside. The officers knew that there were pie stains on the wall and asked for him. She told a lie. "He doesn't live here." I filed a complaint on him anyway.

The next day, Pat brought him back into the house as if nothing happened. I asked if she was crazy. She didn't answer me. I called Mom collect. Of course, and she complained about her phone bill being high. I then made a promise to myself that when I got a job, I would pay the bill.

Mom didn't want to hear what happened and I didn't understand. I was tired of being mistreated and I wanted out, away from her, to never look back. Living with Pat and her boyfriend was a living nightmare. I had made up my mind on how to survive in this world filled with hatred. The tool was to finish school and go off to college rather than being homeless.

Met Luis during my junior year of high school while I was walking home from school. He was a very nice guy and never pushed me into anything and was very patient. He would have me come over to his mother's house and watch TV with him and his mother who didn't speak English. He was very pleasant to be around and had a lot of respect for women. After our movie nights, he would send me home in a cab. He was a good friend, but unfortunately, our friendship ended abruptly. His mother became ill, and she went back to Puerto Rico, and he went along with her to help care for her. I was used to disappointment, so I was hardly affected by it.

# CHAPTER TWENTY-EIGHT

A friend of my mom referred us to a friend that was going to help us get our green cards. We had to provide two thousand dollars each and two photo ideas. He took the money up front and said that he would come back to retrieve our passports. The process was taking too long and I was worried. We would call this friend to check the status and contact her own mother with no results.

I used one of Pat's friends to call this person and impersonated himself as a detective. He denied knowing me and told the "detective" that he was busy fixing his house. When he was told that he scammed us, he hung up on us and changed his number. We both forgave her mother for what she did. To this day, we don't understand why it happened.

# CHAPTER TWENTY-NINE

Pat's boyfriend became more controlling, meaner even. I would come home from school and would find my underwear in the toilet! Sometimes, he would flush them right in front of my face just to get me angry. I just couldn't cry anymore, I became harder. I called my sister Pat and told her what happened and she laughed. I was running out of underwear to wear to school. I resorted to hand-washing the few I owned for school.

Pat realized my birthday was coming up and tried to ask her boyfriend what I liked. She eventually asked me what I wanted, and I told her a dog because I loved animals. I was watching TV that day about dogs that needed adoption so I asked my sister about going there to get one myself.

The shelter was in New York, and my friend from high school went with me. We didn't have enough money so we took our lunch money and caught the train. Prior to leaving, I asked my sister Pat for some more money, but she said that I had enough, so off we went! We got the puppy and caught the train back to Penn Station and realized my sister Pat lied about having enough money. We didn't know what to do so I decided to walk home with the dog. One hour and fifteen minutes later, on the way back, my shoes fell apart from walking so much. My feet were burning but I didn't want to give up. I was missing the sole from my right shoe, but I made it home with the dog I called Rex.

Everyone fell in love with this dog. He was therapeutic for us all. Unfortunately, that didn't last long, my sister was upset that all my focus was on the dog than her and her boyfriend. I needed to heal. I wanted peace in my life. A month later, Pat turned on me once again. She wanted me out of her house and I asked, "Why? What have I done?"

Pat threw me out of her house. She didn't care how I will live or survive, but I wouldn't move. She actually grabbed me by the last bra I had in my name, the only bra I had, tearing it off and out went the dog and myself. I had no place to go, so I decided to just walk back and forth up and down the street until I got tired and I did not care anymore. I had the dog with me, and he looked as if he felt sorry for me. It snowed that day, so hard. I had Jheri curls in my hair that were dripping. The droplets from my hair fell with the snowflakes as they melted upon my face.

I didn't want to live anymore.

Mom didn't believe me when I called her for help, and she closed all the doors on me. Pat tried to break my bond with Mom by telling lies on me. She told Mom that I wasn't doing well in school, and she saw me with some strange guy. It was crazy. All I wanted to do was graduate from school and never come back. Pat wanted me to fail, but her efforts to bring me down only made me stronger. I got so tired walking back and forth thinking about where I was going. After my walk, I returned home and Pat had all my clothes on the porch where everyone could see.

A classmate that lived around the corner from me happened to walk by and see all my clothes. She asked me what happened. After my explanation, she decided to ask her mom if I could stay with her for a while, just so I could finish school. I wanted her to take my dog rather than myself because I didn't want him to suffer like I did.

# CHAPTER THIRTY

J anet had nine sisters living in a three-bedroom apartment in the projects. The place was big enough to hold three beds and a cot, which I ended up having. Janet was the second friend I had in high school, but she had the kindest heart. She was from Trinidad. Janet's oldest sister was put in charge of the household and told me I could stay and finish school. I felt alive again, but my dog couldn't stay.

I had to walk the dog outside around the projects and let him go. It was the most painful thing I had ever done. I abandoned him, just like my family did, and I never got over it. I had to run inside to hide from him, hoping that someone would take him.

I could hear his yelps of sadness, but someone did take him in. I whispered, "You're in good hands now, and I am sorry." I never looked back after seeing him happy with that family. I never knew that it would be so painful, knowing the journey I took from the animal shelter, and the cry of Rex. I felt chills going through my body. His cry was agonizing to hear, and I cried harder on the inside. I loved him so much and I believed he was human. Could you imagine that pain?

Once I settled in at my friend's place, I went to visit another classmate, Gina. I just wanted her to know that I was okay. She didn't know what was going on because I never spoke about what I was going through. I had one more year in high school, and I was living with Janet for about a month now.

Gina was different from Janet. She was soft-spoken, peaceful, loving, and her spirit was bright. She would make you feel as if you could accomplish anything, including her mother, Perk. I didn't share much details about my current situation, I never did. Gina had no clue that I was homeless and living with friends. They didn't know what was going on because I didn't trust anyone, so I sat there in their house just listening to the family I just loved to be around.

It was time for me to go back to my other house so I wouldn't get locked out. I would usually be in the house before 8:00 p.m. I didn't want any excuse to be on the street again. I had no money and no food, but a family who welcomed me with open arms. I respected them so much. They made me part of their family—something I had not had in a long time. They offered me a plate of food every day, and I felt so guilty like I was taking food out of their mouths so I decided that I would eat less while I was there. I would make dumplings out of flour and boil and fry them to eat with jelly. Janet's oldest sister would ask me if I ate, and I would lie and tell her, "Yes, I did."

The pain from the gas in my stomach would be unbearable at times, and I would drink tea every night in efforts to stop the pain. I would sit on the ledge of the ninth-floor window of the apartment wondering, *Why me?*

# CHAPTER THIRTY-ONE

I didn't want to go out, so I stayed home more often now. My friend Janet wasn't doing too well in school, and I couldn't help her because she missed too many days of school. She was told that she would not be allowed back unless she had a doctor's note for those days. Janet had an abusive boyfriend who kept her from school.

After living there for about two or three months, I decided to grab newspaper. We needed jobs and quick! I found a babysitting job for my friend and she had an interview, but she was so afraid of her boyfriend, so I pretended to be her on the phone. The lady ended up giving her a face to face interview, but when she refused to go, I went after the job myself. I met the family with four kids. The family asked why a young girl like me wanted to babysit all these children. I told them that I wanted a job so I could have food to eat and that I loved kids.

I got the job. That was the best thing that ever happened. It wasn't a lot but grateful was the word, and I thanked God for holding me together. On my way back, I told Janet that I had news for her. I told her that I got the job and immediately after sharing the good news, Janet's oldest sister told me that I had to leave. I was told that I couldn't stay with them anymore because my sister wanted me back home. Reality set in for me.

I needed help. *Help!*

My soul, it felt as if it was leaving my body. I was empty on the inside. I begged for mercy, to stay just a little while longer. My friend Janet came to me and told me that Pat, my own sister, paid her sister to throw me out. My sister became friends with Janet's sister and would secretly call her every night.

# CHAPTER THIRTY-TWO

With nowhere to go, I got packed and kissed everyone goodbye and never looked back again. I went home and I wanted to see if Pat really wanted me back home, but she already had a few friends living with her. They watched her as she mistreated me and one of her friend's decided that was not a place for her, and left that night.

I only had four months left in school, but in the two weeks of my return to my sister's place, things had changed. Pat knew she didn't want me there and had another plan of her own. I came home from school, opened the door, and all the furniture and everything else she owned was gone. The only thing that was left was my green suitcase filled with my clothes sitting in the middle of the floor.

I didn't cry because by this time, I was used to the let down and the rejection. I did not expect happiness. I grew more hatred toward my sister, but I also prayed so hard that my heart started to hurt. I had to stay strong for Mom, of course.

I couldn't think, but I couldn't stay there, either. My only option was to call my only friend, Gina, from a phone that I hid outside to secretly call my mother when there were problems. Luckily, the phone was not cut off just yet. I had to take a moment to take everything in.

I watched the windows, staring through them mostly, as the curtains blew in and out somberly. I took a deep breath and placed that call to Gina and told her what Pat did. She cried and called me a liar, but she came to the house in a second with her mom. I had no more emotions; they died that day.

# CHAPTER THIRTY-THREE

Perk, Gina's mom, was furious. She called my sister crazy. She claimed that Pat could have gotten into trouble with the law for what she did, but Perk ended up saving me from all the trouble. Perk called Mom and informed her that very day. Mom was upset with the news, and she quickly reached out to Pat to find out what was going on.

One day, Pat and Janet showed up at Perk's house where I was staying and wanted to talk to Perk. What little effort that was made was only an attempt to convince Perk to kick me out of her home. They both stated that I ran up both of their phone bills with no evidence of either accusation.

Perk, who was a secretary at the school at that time, told Pat how wicked of a sister she was and asked her what she wanted from me. Perk ran them out of her house and just having someone that believed in me was the greatest victory God could have done for me. It saved my soul from falling deeper into the darkness. I was able to smile and have her as a mother, and I bonded with them, my family. My soul was now at ease.

I could see the anger seeping from within Pat due to her failed attempt to ruin my life. Her lies caught up to her, and God proved he was in charge. I was finally able to close my eyes and find some kind of peace.

# CHAPTER THIRTY-FOUR

It was graduation time and well, we made it, both Gina and me. I helped her study so we both would succeed as sisters. I inhaled and looked at her. What a struggle at first. She didn't think she was going to make it, being pregnant in her last year of high school.

Prom time crept around, and I was always shy. I didn't go out on dates or really talk to guys because I didn't think I was pretty enough, but someone did ask me to go. I was afraid ask Pat, so instead, I asked Mom. I called her one afternoon after school and she agreed. She told me she would pick extra peanuts to sell in order to make the money I needed to get a dress. She sent the money to Cynthia, and Cynthia brought the prom dress and sent it to Pat. I was reassured that the dress would be one of the kind, or at least I would be the only one wearing the dress as my dress would be coming all the way from New York. Pat called sister Cynthia for a prom dress, and she sent the ugliest black dress I had ever seen. I was fit for a ball or a funeral or both. My heart sank; I just wanted a simple dress. I decided to call Mom, but I didn't want to ask her for money to buy a dress. Mom told me that she was sending Cynthia fifty dollars every week for me, but my sister never told me. When I finally asked, her response was, "I support you."

I hated her for taking money from Mom because of the lengths she had to go to earn money from farming. My heart started to ache again just knowing that she profited money from her from the very first day of my arrival. I didn't bother going to prom because graduation was more important to me. I invited both of my sisters just to show them that they had knocked me down in so many ways, but I still stood strong and made it without them.

Both sisters came to the graduation, and they both ended up in the bathroom with their shoes off, fighting. Pat had invited her boyfriend, and no one wanted him to be there, especially me. It was my time. Gina had called me into the bathroom. I was told that my sisters were fighting, hitting each other with shoes. I had to break it up and then walk away to march.

Cynthia wanted me to go back to New York with her after graduation, but I was already accepted into a college in New Jersey. I had no intention or interest to be with either of them. Pat told me Mom told her to care for me. Her kids had pulled me aside and whispered to please help them that her boyfriend was beating them up. I always had a soft spot for kids, so I couldn't say no. They looked helpless.

I told them I wouldn't be home that much. I had to tell my sister Cynthia I was going back for the kids' sake. She didn't understand what was going on and I never told her. Instead, she told me to take her shoes off that she bought me on graduation day and made me walk barefoot, which I did.

I said thank you.

# CHAPTER THIRTY-FIVE

P at and her boyfriend rented a house in Union, so we drove off without any shoes on my feet. I said goodbye to Perk and got ready for four years of college in Teaneck. I had no money, no backup plan, but I wanted to go to school and help people.

My nightmare came when Pat's boyfriend became controlling. He rented the house so he told her to make sure his food was cooked before going to church, otherwise, he would throw us out. I didn't care for Pat or her boyfriend; I had a life, a future that I was trying to achieve.

I had the same boyfriend that I hung onto for about three years. I met Andre in my sophomore year at a candy store. I was afraid to date him. I had him as a boyfriend but never engaged with him as one because I kept what my mother taught me in my head. If you kiss a boy, you will get pregnant, and I believed it. I would always hide from him because he was seven years older and wanted me to love him fast.

He never gave up on me, but when he asked me to marry him, he never had a ring to back it up, so I never took him seriously about anything. I share a little bit about my personal life with him, but I didn't want pity from him. One thing I shared with him was that Cynthia had filed for me to become a citizen but canceled my paperwork so I was stuck in the States. I couldn't do what I wanted with school, but I still went off to college, and he drove me there to and from.

I was nineteen years old now going to school. I fell in love with this guy who had been by my side from day one. I had ended up sleeping with him for the first time as a virgin. I didn't know anything about sex, and I ended up pregnant with my daughter. I was so upset. I wasn't ready for motherhood. All I knew was that I was lost. This was one thing I just wasn't ready for, but I always believed in God and prayed a lot. I had faith, so I decided to keep her.

I didn't tell Pat.

While I was in college, the dean called me in his office and told me I was a great student, but my financial aid papers had not been received. I told him that it was sent out a long time ago in order for me to be here. Summer break came and all the students had to go home. Naturally, my boyfriend wanted to take me home because he knew I was carrying his firstborn child, but that was a secret I kept for about three months.

Pat had no idea I was carrying until she made the mistake of yelling at me. She wanted me to go to the store for her boyfriend to buy bread and milk. I asked her for the money and she sent me into her bag. There, right before my eyes, were my financial aid papers.

Pat never sent them out. She had taken my dreams away.

I told my boyfriend. He wanted me to live with him and I said no. We weren't married, and I didn't want that kind of life—unwed with more babies. I confronted Pat about my papers.

She screamed so loud, "*Why did you go in my pocketbook?*"

I reminded her that she had sent me in her back and that was when I saw my papers with my name on it. It was *my* future!

Pat didn't care. She was angry because I found out she was a liar and could never be trusted. I finally told her about being pregnant, knowing I was three months in, but I was happy just knowing that I was becoming a mother and I would have someone to love me.

Pat couldn't stand the news, but I told her not to tell Mom because I wanted to be the one to tell her myself. She waited until I left to go out that evening, called Mom, and told her a bunch of lies. I lost my mother for over a year, begging for forgiveness.

"Please don't turn your back on me at this time, I have suffered enough, Mom. Please help me, Mother!" Mom slammed the phone down in my ears. My spirit was so low it nearly left my body. I had to pull myself together for the baby's sake. I didn't care about what Pat had to say any longer. All I wanted was a healthy baby.

I was still living in the abusive household with my sister and her boyfriend. The boyfriend became more abusive toward the kids, verbally, and he tried to hit Rosalind with an elephant statue. He was upset with her because she didn't want to go to the store for him. As big as I was at that stage of my pregnancy, I got up and told him to leave my sister and her kids alone. He was angrier with me and called the police stating that there was a witch in the back room and he wanted me out of the house. The officer came and looked at him. He asked if he was okay since the only thing he saw was a pregnant female ready to give birth soon. The officer told him, "Have a great night," and told him not to call again.

It was a whole lot of stress that came off my chest because I wanted to show Pat how to be a parent. You're more vulnerable and you don't want to mistreat your child like I was mistreated. I didn't have a job, but I was getting help from her father. Pat also helped because she could control my life more now that I had the baby. It gave her more power. I got help from the state for my child. He made me drop it because he didn't want his child using government assistance. I was always afraid of him because he was tall and skinny. He never wanted me to wear certain clothes, lot top shirts, and jean pants that showed my shape.

He was controlling. He would put a gun in my mouth and play with the trigger when I was pregnant so I wouldn't look at other men. He would torment me. *Click, click* noise.

# CHAPTER THIRTY-SIX

My child, Chanelle, was born. She was my laughter. My pain had been hidden so deep, you couldn't hurt me anymore, and I became even stronger. Chanelle was the peace for the family. The pain was gone from the house. I thought I would never see another day of drama until my daughter was about three years old. Pat's boyfriend started throwing food on the walls again, and we were all thrown out.

I thought him and Pat had purchased the house together, but I found out later it was all a lie again. Here we go again. Pat came from church and found all her stuff on the street. She was shocked and begged him to let her back in, but this time, he meant it. Pat found another house, three bedrooms upstairs and downstairs in Union. It wasn't in great shape at all. We were there for at least three years, and then someone bought the house from right under her.

Pat wanted a house so badly that she knew she couldn't afford. She ended up getting another house for rent. The light got cut off in the winter, and it felt like we were sleeping outside. It felt like my heart was on ice; I needed fire to warm my soul. I decided to let the baby stay with her dad, and I stayed with Pat because I was trying to be a humble and loving person—something that she would never be. I chose to suffer with her because I needed to be accepted.

# CHAPTER THIRTY-SEVEN

I got a restraining order from her father because he became more violent and wanted to take my child away. He would take her and would fail to bring her home at the time agreed with visitation. I called the police, and he was escorted along with my child to the house to bring her back.

Around the same time, I was given a book with poems from a college friend that had love poems to read and Pat gave the book to my child's father thinking that the poems were written for me. He took me into the car and drove me to a dead end street. He locked all the doors and asked me about the book. He didn't believe me when I explained, and he grabbed my face and squeezed harder. And then I rolled the window down and crawled out and ran home.

# CHAPTER THIRTY-EIGHT

My youngest brother came up for vacation and stayed with us. I used to keep a diary about myself, expressing my thoughts and my dreams and I wrote about my love. My brother and sister found and read my diary. I caught them as they were laughing at the words in my diary. I grew angrier and it carried over throughout my life.

I wanted out of this house and I packed a few of my things each day. I had no way to go, but it encouraged me to make a move. I was getting older, and my friends from college would laugh at me whenever I told them stories. They thought they were jokes, but it was my life. It felt good to be able to turn my pain into laughter and that is how I managed to survive.

Pat found a job for me working with her at a nursing home. I was working in dietary. It felt good having your own. It wasn't enough, but I was gaining my independence, at least that's how I saw it. I worked there for ten years, and Pat threatened me and stated that if I didn't give her all my checks and tell everyone that the house was hers, she would throw me out. I couldn't stand lying and it bothered me for such a long time. I didn't trust anyone enough to tell them that I was being abused.

Pat wasn't a nice person at all. She used to pay people at my job to spy on me and count the number of hours I worked. I was so sick to my stomach. How could she do that? I kept one particular woman close to me that she was paying until I was about to leave Pat's house for good.

Pat told these people at work that she loved to see me beg.

What a heartless sister Pat turned out to be. She had power over my life for so long, but I asked God for guidance to leave her house so I could find some much needed peace once again.

# CHAPTER THIRTY-NINE

Pat asked her male friend, a new guy, to help her get a car. She had no driver's license. She got into her new car to take me to work and when she got into a car accident that day, she totaled her car. The officer came. He was a very sweet man, older, and his main concern was our safety. He never asked for the driver's license of my sister's because he was worried about our injuries. He sent for an ambulance, and when they came, Pat told me to say that I couldn't breathe, to say that I needed oxygen when, in fact, nothing was wrong with me.

The first thought that came to mind were her children, I didn't like the idea of lying, but I also didn't want her to go to jail. So we went to the hospital and with the oxygen mask over my face, I told Pat, "This is wrong, in God's name, this is wrong."

I wanted to get away from her, but I had no place to go because Mom was seventeen hundred miles away from me. I was tired of her lies, and I wanted to run away from her. At the hospital, I couldn't shake the feeling of shame and disgust. I tried to convince her to do the right thing just as the officer came to check on us at the hospital.

For some reason, Pat just couldn't pass the driving test, and after that experience, I caught the bus for a long time. I couldn't afford to buy decent shoes for work, and the slush from the snow would go through my shoes, nearly giving me frostbite, but honestly, I didn't mind because the pain made me think about ways to escape her and how to survive with her lies.

Her "friend" who purchased the car in his name was yelling at her from the phone. All you could hear was the echo, "She is suing for $2,000 dollars in damages." I was only making about $180 every two weeks. I couldn't even afford to help pay the $1,400 a month for rent.

Every time I would get paid, Pat would take all my money. I had to beg her for a couple of dollars to feed my daughter and catch the bus to work, but Pat wanted it all and didn't care how my child ate.

# CHAPTER FORTY

I became friends with one of the coworkers Pat was giving money to. I told her, "Please don't tell Pat about my union allowance because my child needs food and I need a place to live." I was able to save the money I needed and I found out that Pat was going to St. Kitts to visit Mom for two weeks. That's when I walked through Maplewood looking for a place. I found an attic that was turned into a one-bedroom apartment. It didn't have a kitchen sink, but I didn't care. I had my freedom, and I could breathe.

I was already packed for an entire year before I discovered my apartment, and when Pat flew out, I called my girlfriend Ray. Ray was a friend from my college days. She was my inspiration and a great listener. Ray was always careful when talking to me about my family because whenever I started crying, she would too.

I made sure to feed the kids, and I left the day that Pat was expected to fly back into New Jersey; the kids were old enough now to take care of themselves. Ray had a little car that couldn't carry much, but I didn't have much to begin with, so we put my daughter's mattress on top of her car and drove off.

I wrote a letter to Pat telling her, "Thank you for allowing me to stay with you, but it is time for me to be on my own," and she yelled at me, telling me that I would come back and beg that I wouldn't make it. So I made it my intention to survive without her. First night in the apartment: all we had was one spoon, fork, knife, pot, and two cups. My daughter's canopy bed was sitting on the floor. We made a toast that night. I don't think my daughter understood the importance of that night. The beginning of my independence, the beginning of my freedom, but just the same, we clinked our dollar-store glasses and ate Cap'n Crunch cereal on the floor in the kitchen.

We still worked at the same nursing home, and I decided to take my boss with me to return her keys to the house. She had cursed me out so badly you could practically taste the bitterness in her mouth. It scared me, and when I looked over, I saw my boss had a face of disgust.

I had to stop her.

I told her I was living in hell with her for so long and that I was aware that she had stolen my daughter's child support checks and that did it. We never spoke of the situation ever again.

I could have gotten her arrested, but she and Mom asked me to show compassion.

# CHAPTER FORTY-ONE

Going to work one day with my daughter to collect my check. I happened to glance over to see Luis on the same bus! It had been so many years since I had seen him, at least ten to be exact. We talked for a little while, and he looked over at my daughter and jokingly asked me if Chay was his child. I laughed and said, "You must be out of your mind!"

During our talk, he told me that the reason why we lost touch was because he had to go back to Puerto Rico to care for his mother who had cancer. It had been so nice to see him again, and things felt right. I felt like there was a reason why he was brought back into my life, so I went with it.

We decided to start all over again. We planned on getting married and even having a baby! Things were really looking up for me, and it was a very joyous moment in my life until I got pregnant. Luis went away suddenly as his mother became ill again. I couldn't believe the turn of events. How could he leave me like this?

So here I was, stuck. I was pregnant, lost Luis, and was feeling a little lost myself. I was getting tired of calling him. I spent hours of nonstop searching through the yellow pages. My old high school friend would help me drive to the addresses listed in hopes of finding this man once again. After a few months, I decided not to stress and focus on having a healthy baby. It's not that I gave up the search, but I felt my health and the baby's health were far more important.

# CHAPTER FORTY-TWO

I thought everything was over, that the drama subsided as the time went on, but then Pat grinned her sinister smile and told the staff at our job that I didn't have a green card, I lost my job! I had no way to prove that I was indeed a citizen, which resulted in me losing my job. What Pat didn't know was that I was in the process of receiving my green card, it just didn't arrive in time for me to maintain my job, but I kept my silence, creeping along like the clouds in the sky on a slow summer day.

I was pregnant with my second child and yet, that did not matter to my sister because she wanted me to be homeless and beg her to come back. Since losing my job, I did what she expected of me, I fell into her trap, swallowed my pride, and I asked her for a plate of food for myself and my children. I just wanted enough food to sustain my family until I started my new job. She told me that she was going to call me back and hung up.

Pat then called my other sister, Cynthia, and together, they laughed at me. Pat entertained the idea that I could possibly lose my new apartment and that I had no money to care for my children. What a shame as *they* were the ones who did this to me, who caused all this pain.

Shortly after my conversation with Pat, Victor called me and told me that he couldn't take it. He had overheard his mother laughing at me to Cynthia. He wanted me to know how evil his mother was, and he was overwhelmed with guilt.

I called Ray and told her what happened. I just needed a friend to talk to at this point. I wanted someone to hear me out. Together, we prayed on it, and it gave me some relief, a boost of faith that things were going to get better. Hours had gone by, and I heard a car pull up in the driveway. Ray had come over to check on me. She said she wanted to see how I was holding up after our conversation and before she left, she handed me food and money for rent.

The following day, I received my W2 form in the mail. I called Ray and told her that I was grateful for the money, but I would not need it. I gave her money back and immediately filed my income taxes. When the check arrived, I saved the money to cover the next three months' rent.

# CHAPTER FORTY-THREE

I was able to work at that nursing home until the baby was born. I had stopped looking for Luis during that time, but now my child had been born! Simone was about three months old when my boss asked where her father was. He said she is a beautiful child and needs a father in her life. That was when I decided to look for Luis again. I had found ten guys by the name "L. Ibarrondo" in the yellow pages, and I called each and every one. The ninth one seemed right. I called him and told him that he had a daughter. He was *shocked!* He said, "Really? I have been locked up for ten years, and no one told me that I had a child!"

That was the wrong Luis. That conversation scared me. I know it couldn't be him, so I tried one last time. I called the last number, and he finally answered. So I called my girlfriend up and had her drive me to the address. I had two baby bottles premade, three outfits, four pampers, baby wash and lotion, pacifier, and wipes all packed.

I headed over to the apartment and sat in the car and waited to see if he was coming out because I wasn't sure which door was his. But there he was smoking a cigarette with a bag of groceries in his hand. He walked into the building, and I got out of the car and followed him. I stayed a few steps behind and watched him go into the apartment. That's when I found his apartment number. I waited about two seconds, inhaled deeply, and knocked on the door.

He said, "Hello," but I didn't answer. I knocked again. He finally answered the door, reluctantly, until he saw me with the baby in my hands.

"You have been missing for a while, I didn't do this without you. Get to know your child. This is your daughter, Simone Brianna."

I handed him the baby along with her baby bag and gave him four hours to get to know his daughter. He was shocked and said that he didn't know how this was supposed to be his child. I offered a DNA test and told him that he would have to pay for it and I walked away.

Four hours passed, and I came back to his apartment and he was crying like crazy. He called his family, especially his sister, and told them he had a daughter. He wanted me to give up Simone and walk away. He said that she looked too Puerto Rican. I told him to find the Puerto Rican father of the child and let me know who he was. I told him to get a DNA test, and he just kept on crying because he knew it was his child. He also said that he had girlfriends before and believed that he couldn't have kids.

We stayed in contact, and he came over nearly every other day including the weekends.

Eventually, as time went on, he began visiting daily. He was a proud father, and he loved his little girl. They did everything together.

After Simone was two years old. We decided on marriage and we lived together. We were married at my best friend's church, Peaceful Zion Baptist. We paid the clerk 150 dollars. Rachel, Gina, and my kids were the only ones there until the church choir decided to join us. It was a very special moment to me. It was already a small family that came together, all the people that mattered to me here in New Jersey. I didn't think things could get any better until they all came from the lower level singing gospel songs in celebration of our union. We exchanged our vows, and everyone there held hands and said a prayer before we parted ways.

My family never wanted to see anything good come out of me and always wanted me to fail, and I do believe that is why they didn't come but that didn't matter to me. Having them there would have ruined my beautiful day.

# CHAPTER FORTY-FOUR

After losing my job of ten years, I felt like it was time for me to get my license. Although it wasn't the best time to think about getting a car, I needed some motivation. I needed something to keep me going. It worked! Once I got my license, I found a new job, but I soon grew tired of leaving my apartment at 4:00 a.m. to catch the bus just so I could be at work for 8:00 a.m.

It was now time to look for a car. I felt as if I was running myself ragged by these early mornings. I knew a car would allow me more sleep and even the potential for a second job to make additional money. I liked the idea of not having to depend on friends and family for rides. Although I was working at a hospital part-time, I felt powerful; I felt strong.

So the day came when I bought my first car, thanks to Luis's help. It was a 1999 red Honda Civic. I drove it for about seven months and that was when I saw the possibility to pick up a second job. I did so for a little while, working two part-time positions until I was offered a full-time job at the hospital. That was when my car started giving me trouble. Every day it would stop on the highway, and I would have to carry a jug of water to pour on the overheated car.

It was my first car, and I was so proud to have something to drive my girls around. I couldn't fathom the idea of losing it, but she finally died out in the snow. An ambulance saw that my children and I were in the car not far from the house and offered to help. The EMTs carefully pushed my vehicle from the rear very slowly until we reached the front of my apartment. It was time to say goodbye to my very first car.

# CHAPTER FORTY-FIVE

Since things were going well in my life, I finally had the courage to call Dad. I wanted to ask him about myself, to ask him why he mistreated me. I wanted to know if all of those horrible things my sisters had been saying were true.

I woke up from having a dream about a wedding. It was strange dream because Dad was in it. I hadn't seen him since I was a kid! I wanted to talk to him so badly, and as I approached him, I woke up suddenly. Pat was calling me. She told me she had something important that she needed to tell me. She told me Dad had died and that he died of grief. I didn't understand what she meant by that, but I needed answers. I asked what happened to him, and she told me she didn't know.

I couldn't go to St. Kitts because my papers had not been completed. Pat and Cynthia went to the funeral, and I was not mentioned as one of his children as was told by one of my nephews. I was so desperate to find out why he had never spoken a word to me. I still wanted to know how he died and why at such a young age. Pat and Cynthia told the family that Dad had died of grief and everyone believed it to be true for years. Later I found out, while Pat was talking to Cynthia, that Dad actually had cancer, but the two of them wanted that to remain a secret.

When Pat let the truth slip from her lips, I took the opportunity to tell my mother the truth. She was so hurt! I do believe at one point she believed he passed from grief. My two oldest siblings had no clue how abusive Dad was toward the both of us because they weren't around yet they had spread rumors about Mom and said that Mom had killed Dad. Her own children had manipulated her and the rest of the family through lies. She cried to me, asking the world how her children could be so wicked, shocked that her kids were accusing her of something so evil.

I never thought I would ever hear my mother cry. Such a strong woman she is. Hearing your own mother cry is a burden too heavy for one to carry. All I could do for her was pray.

# CHAPTER FORTY-SIX

I had loved the idea of being a married woman until I happened to get up out of bed one morning. Something came over me, I was watching him with one eye open and one eye closed. Something just didn't feel right. I was unaware of a lawsuit settlement from a car accident that he had before we rekindled things. I caught him on the computer going through his e-mails. When we went to work, he forgot to close the e-mail, and that's when I saw he purchased a three-family house without me knowing, so I played along.

Suddenly, Luis would argue with me for the smallest things. He would refuse to move his car at night to adhere to the parking signs and when he was ticketed, he would come home screaming at me, blaming me for the ticket. Then one day, he asked me for our child's social security, and when I told him no, we had a nasty fight. He got up and told me that he was leaving me, so I helped him by throwing his clothes down the stairs because it seemed as if he wanted me to throw him out anyway so he could move into his new house. I was one step ahead of him. I knew where the house was located and kept that information stored. After years of separation, he became less of a father and found interest in one of his new neighbors.

# CHAPTER FORTY-SEVEN

I had to find a way to help Mom to see how strong and independent I became. I had become so strong and respectful to my mother and loved her. She raised me into who I was. I just wished she had caught me when I was falling. I wished she had kept those doors open for me. To this day, I still hurt, but I understand she had been drowning herself from the abuse of losing her life partner. Mom will sleep in her partner's room at times then go back to her room to sleep. It was a comfort for her missing her partner of so many years.

I made a choice to have positive people in my life, but not too many, just three good friends, and I was happy. I had been talking to my childhood buddy that I grew up with, and I fell in love with him after going back and forth to see him at the age of forty-one. The older women from Mom's generation began telling me that I looked just like my father. I was confused by this because Dad was half Caucasian. He never allowed me to call him Dad and never acknowledged me as his daughter.

Mom was so angry that I was dating someone from the island. You would have thought I was dating a murderer! She disapproved of the relationship and threatened to take away the house she had left for me in her will. I didn't care one bit. I took the chance to live and be happy, and that's when my mother decided to stop talking to me. Mom thought that her kids were too good to be with someone who couldn't provide wealth or financial stability.

# CHAPTER FORTY-EIGHT

I made plans to marry my childhood sweetheart as poor as he was, no matter what Mom thought about it. He had a heart of gold and accepted me for who I was. Nothing else was important.

As I was standing on his porch, I watched this tall, black guy about seven feet tall, riding a bike, yelling. I looked at him and smiled. He said, "Good morning." But what came to mind was his bike. The tires had cut up tennis balls all along the spikes—something I did to my own bike as a kid. It was something so I could see at night. Whenever you pedaled fast, the wheels would light up.

I blinked from my daydream and realized that mysterious guy was still looking at me, so I got up and went inside. Later that day, my fiancé came home from work, and I told him what happened. He nodded and said, "Maybe that was for you." Unsure of what he meant, I let it go, maybe he wasn't listening. He didn't seem very interested in what happened anyway.

Later that evening, the same guy came back and called out to my fiancé. He walked over to the gate and let himself in. My fiancé then introduced me to the guy, saying that it was his friend. He said that the guy wanted to talk to me. The guy then asked me if my name was Charmane Nisbett. I responded, "Yes, why?" He then went on to say that he was my brother.

I asked him who was his father and he said Palmer. I shook my head and told him that Nisbett was my father, and when I looked over at my fiancé, he said, "Charm, it's true."

I was shocked, embarrassed, and I wanted to get out and try to catch my breath. This random guy had so much information about me and said that his dad had told him all these things before he died. He said to me that I looked like his older sister, Kima, and that we had the same smile. His hands was dripping with sweat that I had to tell him to calm down and relax.

I thought I was in a dream, and I was fighting to wake up. I was looking over at my partner, and I realized that he was in on this. How long had he known this? My fiancé told my alleged brother when I was coming and going between the island. I couldn't sleep.

I had so many questions, but I was so embarrassed, and I wanted to turn my back away from St. Kitts forever. In this moment, it was confirmed that I didn't know anything about myself. I couldn't trust anyone anymore. How could my family be so disloyal and not tell me the truth? I was so alone and drained.

I felt that the entire world lied to me, including my now husband. Who am I?

I decided that I didn't want anything to do with that country anymore. It brought me too many painful memories and a lot of embarrassment. I didn't want to be a fool to anyone, and I ran back to the United States in agony. I didn't want anything to do with the man I loved and married. After two years had passed, two years of me ignoring him, I sent him the divorce papers and never looked back.

He was my other half, but I felt as if he was just like the rest of the dishonest people that kept me in the dark. How could he keep such a big secret from his own wife?

# CHAPTER FORTY-NINE

I went to the island just to talk to Mom because I would write letters and call her on the phone and she would never answer. Mom insisted that if I were to show up at her doorstep, she would throw hot water in my face. Needless to say, I was scared. I loved her, but I also needed answers. I wanted to know what was going on because a random guy came up to me and told me that he was my brother. When I told her of the incident, she wanted to know who the person was and simply avoided my questions.

I knew something didn't add up so I asked her if her husband, Mr. Nisbett, was my father. She told me, "If he is not your father, go look for yours." One of her friends happened to see me at the beach, and she said that she didn't know me, that she only knew of my mother having thirteen children, not fourteen.

The few people who knew me, knew she had a dark secret, and they never wanted it to resurface, hoping it would be carried to the grave.

# CHAPTER FIFTY

Luis reached out to me. I don't know if it was his own guilt or the shame he was getting from his family that he decided to try to come back into our daughter's life, but he did. I am a very forgiving person, and I like looking at the bigger picture. I realized the best thing to do was allow him back into Simone's life. There was no reason why she should be punished for his wrong doings, and after a while, Luis and I became friends once again.

Christmas Day was his day as it was their favorite holiday to spend together. He always made sure he would never miss Christmas no matter how things were with the two of us for his daughter's sake. The doorbell rang, and I opened it expecting to see Luis but was greeted by an undercover officer who served papers for our divorce. I couldn't believe the way in which he handled this. I thought we could have discussed this without the presence of an officer, especially on Christmas Day.

I took the papers, closed the door, and called Luis. He needed to know that I was ready and willing to let him go, but his approach was uncalled for. He told me that he discussed the way things went with us to his neighbor, and she convinced him that it was time to move on. I didn't fight or argue about it, I just let it be. I signed those papers and tried to move on with my life.

Things turned sour very quickly after that. Simone was spending time with her father, as usual, but something was different, and I couldn't put my finger on it, not right away. Simone came home one day and told me that although she was going to spend the day with her dad, he would often take her to a neighbor's home, just a few houses away from his own house.

I started to believe this was the neighbor that convinced Luis of the divorce, but could she have been strategically working on her own intentions?

I questioned Luis about his neighbor, and he made it seem like he and this other woman were just friends. Something wasn't sitting right with me. I didn't think he was giving me the whole truth, so I patiently waited for more information. After asking Simone where this woman's home was located, I drove by to see that Luis had his car parked in her driveway. I asked around and confirmed that he indeed lived with this woman. I wasn't concerned about Luis moving on, as we are all entitled to do so; I just wanted the truth because I wanted to be certain that our child was safe.

So as time went on, I was being told by Simone and her father that she was not allowed to bring her own snacks into the other woman's house. I then got involved. I felt as if I has to remind Luis that he couldn't allow anyone to mistreat our child. He simply had nothing to say on the matter and every weekend was the same thing. Simone was being told to leave her snacks in her father's car, but things were soon to change.

My daughter had found a business card on the floor of their home and gave it to me. She innocently wanted to show me what the neighbor had looked like. So I thanked her and took the card. I stepped out and I called the number on the card and told that woman not to mess with my child. She questioned how I managed to contact her and when I tried to call her again a few days later, I found out that she changed her cell and house number.

Luis came to my job a few days after my conversation with his girlfriend, yelling and screaming at me, telling me that I disrespected the woman. It didn't bother me, nor was I afraid. My child's safety was my primary concern, and I could see that he lost sight of that.

# CHAPTER FIFTY-ONE

One hot summer day in July, my eldest daughter's birthday to be exact, I received a call from Chanelle crying. I could barely make out what she was saying. I had to tell her to calm down and try to explain herself slowly. She told me that someone had called the police and said that my youngest daughter was jumping up and down in the street saying that she was hungry. The police answered the anonymous call and came to the apartment to check the refrigerator to verify if there was any truth to the story. Chanelle said they showed their badge, asked to come in, and went straight into the kitchen. After asking if Simone had been outside, they left.

It hit me like a ton of bricks. I knew Luis and his new girlfriend had something to do with this. When I came home, I personally spoke with a gentlemen working from Child Protective Services. He told me that the call was suspicious because the person who called in anonymously "knew the child's exact spelling of her first middle and last name as well as her address."

He insisted that I should file a complaint on them both, but instead, I confronted Luis. I didn't like the idea of things getting any messier than they were. He apologized and said that it wasn't him, that it was her and thought that placing a call like that would help get him custody of Simone. I wasn't too upset with him after our talk because it was then that I realized that he did not have common sense. He obviously was not thinking clearly.

Unfortunately for me, that meant that she had him exactly where she wanted him. She believed that he had a lot of money, and she was trying to get him to divorce me and marry her. When I asked him about his neighbor again, I made it clear to him that she was intentionally destroying the relationship that he had with his daughter as he was seeing less and less of her. He told me that I was crazy and that I didn't know what I was talking about.

# CHAPTER FIFTY-TWO

Christmas Day rolled around again, another one of Luis's holidays with Simone, but the day he was supposed to get his daughter, he never called or showed up. Our first thought was that something was terribly wrong, and the second was that we didn't have any gifts! It was always Luis's responsibility to buy her Christmas gifts because he always knew what she wanted, and he understood I usually didn't have extra money to spend.

I couldn't stomach the idea of Simone worried about her father and having a terrible Christmas, so I took two hundred dollars out of my rent to buy her gifts, and while I was out, I decided to drive to his house. Both houses were vacant, not a single light or car in sight as if they went on vacation. So I went back home and wrapped those gifts and put them under the tree. I could barely stand to look at my daughter's face. It made me feel so hollow inside. I could see she had so much love for her father and was truly concerned.

Hours went by and then the doorbell rang. Chanelle went downstairs to answer the door. It was a faculty member from Simone's school. He handed her a black garbage bag full of brand-new toys. As Chanelle tried to explain what she was doing with the bag, the doorbell rang once more. She took the bag and hid it in the closet and went back downstairs, I could hear her laughing and grew curious and started walking down. She popped her head up and showed me the two additional garbage bags of toys.

Somehow, the school selected her and few others to receive gifts from Santa. She had so many gifts, too many, that she handpicked which ones she wanted to give away to her cousins. Simone was very grateful of all she had received that she wanted to give back, but the only thing she wanted most was her dad to be there on Christmas Day.

A week after Christmas, Simone's dad called and said he was coming to get her. I didn't know what to say. I think I was so shocked that he called as if he wasn't missing for seven days that I just grunted and packed her bag. But when she came home, for the first time, I felt I wasn't properly equipped to handle her emotions. She was screaming at me telling me that her dad got married to the same woman that she felt didn't like her—the neighbor.

Simone had seen the wedding photos that were hidden behind the garbage can. Luis was wrong, and I had to let him know. There was no reason to keep his marriage a secret and that hiding it was only hurting the relationship he had with his daughter. He could have at least informed her or even included her in it. He told me that he wanted to tell her when she became a teenager. I can't imagine keeping a secret from your own child for so long, and I hated him for doing that to her.

Simone became so angry, her exterior toughed like calloused hands. She wouldn't let his wife mistreat her so she told her father that he should spend time with his wife and cut their weekends shorter. She didn't want her father to have to choose between her or his wife. I think she feared what his decision would be if he indeed had to choose, so she chose for him.

One Saturday morning, her father came to pick her up and took her to their house. I always instilled in my children that they shouldn't eat from strangers, something that my mother taught me. So when Simone would visit her father, she would refuse to eat any-thing, especially because she felt as if she was being mistreated but couldn't explain in her own little words as yet. I got a call from Luis later that day, and he told me that they all went out to a restaurant to eat and Simone was going to bring a plate of food home because she didn't eat while they were there. It was shrimp with rice, a simple meal she normally would not refuse, but something in me told me to open up the container of food, and when I did, I saw that there was dog hair in the middle of this container. Now, to be clear, this was not just a single accidental hair that made its way in this container, it was literally a ball of fur as if someone pulled the hairs out from a dog brush and placed it in the center of the plate and mixed it up.

I screamed and called Luis to ask him about the food. I wanted to know why his wife was trying to get my daughter to eat contaminated food. He was shocked and ashamed and kept apologizing over and over. He knew that he lied to me about a restaurant. His wife had prepared the food and tried to serve it to my child.

I decided that was enough.

So I stopped my daughter from going over there because her health and safety was much more important than any relationship she had with her father. I still, to this day, cannot believe that someone could do such a thing to a child. Everything started coming together, and I learned that she was the one who called social services, and that was the last straw for me. I was no longer nice to him.

# CHAPTER FIFTY-THREE

I tried my luck once again and made the decision to lease a new car. It was a gold Honda Civic with beige cloth interior. My eldest daughter loved the car and had planned on taking it as her own when she finished high school. It was early one morning, and I had the kids ready to go to school. We drove a few blocks from home when everything came crashing down. We were going northbound in the right lane when a SUV going southbound whipped an accelerated left turn into my car. The force from the impact was so strong, the car was pushed from the street, into a traffic light, and into a gas station. We stopped a few inches away from a gas pump. Thankfully, the traffic pole saved us from an explosion and possible death as it slowed the car down before possible impact.

Stunned, I sat in the car for a second trying to grasp what had just happened. As I looked around, I gasped. There, right before me, was a reflection of an angel that emerged in the fog of my windshield. It felt as if it was my time to die. I felt as if something was pulling me. I couldn't move right away. There was a force that paralyzed my entire body.

My eldest daughter got out and pulled hard to open the jammed door, unaware that the door was still locked. It took a moment for me to realize that she was yelling at me to unlock the door, and so I did. She pulled her sister out of her car seat, and I slowly got out of the car, and she handed her to me. We were lucky to not have any injuries that day. We were lucky to be alive.

# CHAPTER FIFTY-FOUR

Things became worse with Luis and his wife. He was given freedom from his responsibility as a parent so he could see for himself the type of woman he was dealing with. Years went by, and Luis became very stressed out; he was very mean and yelled more and more. I couldn't hold a conversation with him because he was always yelling, and I knew something was wrong, but I couldn't figure it out. He even stopped speaking to his own mother, which I found to be very unusual since he was a family man.

# CHAPTER FIFTY-FIVE

I wrote Mom another letter letting her know that I felt betrayed by the one person that I looked up to. In that letter, I told her that I forgave her and I still wanted that motherly love. I tried to remind her that we didn't have that much time left to say what was needed.

I am blessed and thankful to have a mother, but I felt as if I was being punished.

Twenty-two years went by before I was able to see my mother after leaving at the age of thirteen. For twenty-two years, I was left in the dark, in an unfamiliar land with strange people. It wasn't until I was nearing my mid-thirties that I was able to see my mother. That was when I received my green card.

Seeing Mom for the first time after years.

Tunde, who was a boss of mine at the hospital that I used to work at, had a friend that was able to sell me a buddy pass so I could see my mother for the first time in years. I was booked for a weekend trip. Tunde told me that I needed to go home and see my mother, and that is exactly what I did. When I landed, I went straight to her house. The roads were exactly the same, so I didn't have difficulty finding the home. I sat there and waited for her to return as she wasn't home. When she finally showed up, she said hello and asked me who I was. That is when I told her, "Well, hello, Mother. It's me, your daughter, Charmane." Her eyes grew wide, showing the whites of her eyeballs. She raised a hand to her mouth in disbelief and barely withheld a curse. She stood there and watched me for a while. She grew pale as if she was seeing a ghost.

Mom's face was much darker than I remembered, perhaps from all the time in the mountains. Her hair was gray, the age showed on her face, and she didn't look like the same person that I remembered. So much time had passed, and there wasn't a single ounce of youth left on her.

Mom had no idea that I was getting my green card so she was surprised to see me. We talked all night, and it seemed as if we were both afraid to go to sleep because we were trying to make up for all the lost time. We didn't want to miss a moment of each other's company. She continuously checked the bedroom that I was staying in to make sure that I was not a figment of her imagination. Every time she came near me, she stared.

During my short stay, I felt as if there was a presence. The door of my bedroom would continuously slam shut. I wondered if it was her husband making himself known.

Visiting her, I tried to make up for all those lost years. Going back down there, I found myself feeling like a teenager all over again. Going home for the first time was like I never left home. I felt good and I felt safe. I started filling Mom in on my life, telling her of the hardships I had experienced like bouncing around from one sister to the other. I told her of the times I babysat Pat's kids while she was at work or out partying. I told her how hard I worked in school, my interest in biology, and my dream to become a nurse.

I will never forget the day that I went home to the island about eight years ago to see Mom for her birthday. Pat wanted to know if I was going, but I didn't have any money. A friend of the family decided to send me a ticket to see Mom. My youngest brother, who lived in Sweden at the time, was there too. On a Sunday, we all went to church with Mom, and my siblings were making a mockery of the church. It had really upset me because I was raised to take religion seriously. When I looked at Mom, she smiled, I didn't know what else to say to them other than stop.

When communion came, all three of us went up to receive it, but Mal had only taken the bread and not the wine. I asked him what was his reasoning for that, and he stated that he didn't know where the church members mouth's had been. He was so rude. When church was over and we were headed home, Pat asked Mal if he wanted to see Dad's grave. It never crossed my mind that Dad would be buried in the same church we attended. I asked Mom why she didn't tell me, and she said it was because she never talked about him. I figured it was best not to ask why she chose that location since he never attended church for as long as I knew him. Pat didn't invite me to see his grave because she knew I wasn't one of them. She knew we didn't have the same father.

My stomach burned at the thought that my oldest siblings knew that I was different.

We were all sitting in the room Dad had considered to be his bedroom when my brother Ivan, who used to be in the army, began telling me how much he missed me and hugged me.

Pat didn't like that. She was jealous and turned to look at me. Pat interrupted our conversation by telling my brother that I wasn't a princess or as innocent as I led on to be. I gave her a look and said, "I never said I was a princess." She was seething with anger and proceeded to making a smacking sound with her tongue as she ate the soup that Mom had made for us.

"You're not a princess. You're not a princess. *You're not a princess!*"

She sent me back to the past. She triggered me and all I wanted to do was pop her in her mouth, but instead, I told her that she needed to tell the family what she did to me. Pat was afraid. She didn't want the truth to come out. She became silent and remained that way for the rest of the day, and when we went back to the States, we never spoke again.

# CHAPTER FIFTY-SIX

One day, I received a phone call at work from Luis, and after a short while, it became a daily situation. He told me that he couldn't sleep, had an upset stomach, and was throwing up constantly with diarrhea. He said that he believed he was getting weak.

During one of those calls, he told me to meet him at Penn Station and I grew worried, but I decided to see him. He asked me to get into the car. Reluctant, I looked over at him and saw he was wearing a hospital gown with a band around his hand. I cautiously went in and before I could even speak, he broke down with his face full of tears. He asked me for my help. He wanted me to care for him. He told me that his wife stole all his money, including the savings he had for our daughter's college. She lied on him and called the police and told them that he hit her and got him arrested for a night shortly after he went into a deep depression, and she changed the locks on the house.

It was after he tried to get back home and realized the locks were changed, he tried to commit suicide and went to see Simone to say goodbye to her. He wanted her face to be the last thing he saw before he died and told me that the pain he felt was unbearable. Simone didn't tell me what happened. I had no idea that this had happened, but he explained everything. He said that Simone was concerned for him and called for an ambulance. They had taken him away, and he left all his belongings with her, which she kept in her room until he got back. My child's father was broken, so I put my feelings aside to help him heal.

# CHAPTER FIFTY-SEVEN

This was going to be one of the hardest things I ever had to do in my life, and I had no idea what I was in for. The second time that Luis committed himself into the hospital, he was directed by his psychiatrist as he was beginning to hear voices. I was going in every day to visit him. I wanted him to know that there were people there who cared about his well-being. On the second day of his admittance, he was given a prescription that he had an allergic reaction to. His left side stiffened, his face contorted and twisted, his jaw locked, and his face was stuck in a snarl. His left arm was stuck in an upright position like a child raising their hand.

I immediately became aware of this reaction, and I yelled at the nurses for help. They tried to tell me that he was committed this way and there was nothing wrong with him. I was so frustrated with this misunderstanding I was having with the head nurse, but she just wasn't trying to hear me out. I was familiar with Luis's situation as I was there when he signed himself into the hospital to get treatment, but the head nurse complained to the doctor and caused more trouble for us all.

I was told that Luis and I were causing problems at the hospital, and they decided that it was best to keep Luis in the hospital for an extra day. This opened my eyes and made me realize that sick people who do not have the support they need tend to get overlooked. They could be misdiagnosed, or just given the wrong prescription that could do more harm than good. Luis really needed the support of a loving family, and I was grateful that I was there to help him.

I lost my voice because I cried so hard. I never felt that kind of pain for anyone. I felt as if God wanted me to do something for him—to save him. I brought Simone with me to visit him, and when he saw her, his face lit up. He told me that she was his motivation to get better. She was his strength. But when she saw him in that manner, darkness grew over her. She had changed. I wanted to heal him so she could have her father back, but little did I know, we were losing her at the same time.

I had to make sure that he ate and took his medication and showered daily. My life had changed, and I was now caring for him as well as my children. I focused my attention on them instead of healing myself. Luis didn't seem to have been getting any better as he told me that the voices told him to put a plastic bag over his head and jump out of the third floor window. He was starting to forget a lot of simple things and was afraid to go outside.

He would leave his hand raised for hours at a time. He would cut himself with his fingernails and pee in the bottle and hide the bottles and lose his bowels and would try to hide the clothes in the attic. There were a times when I saw him with his underwear in his pocket, and that was when I learned that he was soiling himself. I never made him feel like an outcast. I didn't want him to be embarrassed by anything that was happening.

There were times when he would want to drive off the bridge. I felt as if his mind was not on earth. It was somewhere else, but I didn't want him to see that I was afraid, but I would break down whenever I had a moment alone.

Simone became angrier because I was caring for him even after everything that had happened. She became silent and carried her silence for two long years. She believed that after he remarried, he didn't care about her, and she wanted him to be on the street and fend for himself, sick or not. She grew resentful of her father, and she didn't like to see his face.

# CHAPTER FIFTY-EIGHT

There were girls from the island that I was able to reconnect with. We tried to keep each other informed about what was going on in each other's lives as well as any news from the island. One day, one of those old school friends told me that she thought it was best for me to contact another classmate from the past, so he gave the girl my number, and I didn't know what to expect. When I got the call, I was surprised because there were no introductions. The conversation began with the start of two initial questions: if I had dimples and what my full name was.

I wanted to know why she was asking these questions, and that's when she told me that her brother and sister were my brother and sister. I didn't know her and from first impressions, I didn't like her either. I thought she was trying to hurt me.

She was raised by a man named Mr. Palmer. She told me that he had died in her arms sixteen years ago. I was so angry, I cried. I screamed! I didn't want to talk to her anymore. She went on to say that on his deathbed, Mr. Palmer had left a message for me. He told her how much he loved me and how long he had been searching for me. I did not want to hear anymore, and I hung up to call Mom. I begged her to tell me the truth, and she hung up the phone on me.

I wrote Mom a letter asking her to help me that I needed answers this time. She told a family member that I had disrespected her and that she no longer had a daughter by the name of Charmane.

I just wanted to hear the truth from my mother so I could move on. I never thought that I would hear a mother say that she didn't love her own child, but she did.

I forgave her because I needed my mother's love but still, I hoped it wasn't the truth. I kept calling her practically every day for a year straight. She had turned what little family I had against me, but I remained humble. I felt betrayed, helpless, and weak. My heart felt as if it were being stabbed over and over. When I resorted to asking my siblings about the matter, they refused to talk me, but they continued to use me to buy things for them. They didn't care that I had been suffering for so long.

# CHAPTER FIFTY-NINE

One day, I called Mom and one of her friends had answered the phone. He told my mother that she was wrong for not speaking to me. He told me that Mom confided in him and told him that she had indeed slept with Mr. Palmer one time. She wanted it to remain a secret, but why wouldn't you want to tell your own forty-one-year-old daughter? It hurt me to know that she could confide in another person but not me, her child.

Mom didn't think her friend would betray her because she believed in him. All these years, she hoped that she could carry this secret to her grave, but I know it was killing her slowly. I wanted Mom to let go of the secret so she could live peacefully. I wanted to remind her that no matter what, I would always be the child that she once loved. I finally mustered up the courage to contact the family on my real father's side. I wanted to see if there was any truth in all the rumors. I had to go to them because I wasn't getting any answers from Mom. It was a traumatizing experience, painful, and yet confusing. I was afraid that I was going to be rejected again, and I didn't want to face that.

I felt as if Mom threw me away just as Dad did. Mom never wanted me to find love or have friends in St. Kitts because she was afraid her secret would come out about who I really was. One afternoon, a sibling from my mother's side confided in me and told me that the rumors were true and he whispered in my ears that he loved me. I felt as if I was floating through the clouds. My brother told me that he heard Dad tell Mom every morning, "You didn't get rid of that ugly black child yet?" and out of desperation, as a small child, Mom would hide me in a cardboard chicken box and place me under the church next door. She didn't want to upset him because she was worried about what he would do to me.

I grew bitter from knowing the truth and hearing that Dad had thought I was too ugly to be his child. To learn that my mother kept me a secret from the world sent a shocking wave through my body. I felt as if the entire island knew about me except for me. I felt like I was falling with no one to catch me. Who do I belong to, and where do I belong?

# CHAPTER SIXTY

An excerpt from my journal:
"Today, I found myself more involved with my kids' life because we, as parents, need to nourish them and guide them in the world to be humble, honest, loving, and respectful to one another. I want them to know that there are people out there who have been through the worst yet still survived. I am a survivor and here I am at the age of forty-six with two lovely kids who are my life. Both Chanelle and Simone are God's gifted children that put my soul back together.

"They are the reason I am able to live because they believe in me and love me for who I am. I know my kids will become very successful in their lives and will be able to give back to the world, both rich and poor. I want the both of them to keep God first in their lives. Prayer is the goal to achievement and to never give up on your parents no matter what the circumstance is. Love, respect, honor, and treasure them and enjoy what little moment God has planned for us.

"I don't know if I would ever find closure because Mom is eighty-eight now and refuses to speak to me. She cut me out of her life for good. Once again, Pat had won the battle. She brainwashed Mom to get what she wanted: her house and her bankbook. I know she doesn't care for Mom, but God has been watching her every move."

# CHAPTER SIXTY-ONE

I am so grateful for life and for the people who has been there for me and supported me. I decided it was time to search and find out who I was, and since it was a dead end from my mother's side, it was time to go to the source—my brother and sister on my real father's side. I was just so embarrassed because I just didn't see it coming. I was living in a dream, learning that my real father died, and I was his last thought, that his last words were for his child. Knowing that he was searching for me, that he did love me, and tried to protect my mother because he loved her too.

My father and mother made a deal to send me away to another island to be with one of my oldest siblings in St. Croix so Mom's husband wouldn't mistreat me or her badly. I learned that my dimples came from my real father and my heart melted with joy knowing that I belonged to someone and I was loved. Dad had died trying to search for his secret child but with no results. He let himself go. I felt that pain for us both because we didn't get to bond as a father and daughter should.

Dad was kind to all, the sick and the poor; others shared my father's love, and I was robbed of that because Mom was too busy thinking about herself. She didn't consider the child who suffered with her. This is what I learned about my father after I finally made that phone call to my sister, Denise, from my real father's side.

There was a lot of crying and yelling. I wanted so badly to know the truth. She had already accepted me as her sister, and she said she had for a long time. I wanted to know how I slipped through the fingers. Why weren't they there though all my suffering? Denise told me that our father had left instruction before he died to find me and explain that he didn't abandon me when my mother sent me away from St. Kitts.

The overwhelming pain flowed deeper that I cried until there were no more tears left in my body. I was numb and sick of not knowing who I was. She told me that I looked just like him and that I had his mother's dimples—it's the signature of all his children.

It was time to meet her, so I booked my flight to St. Croix for three days. What a nightmare! My niece picked me up from the airport, and I was so shocked at the fact that she could have passed as my own daughter. I was searching for answers, and I was about to learn more than I had expected. I put on a fake smile to conceal the pain I felt inside. I was sad because the truth was staring me in the face, greeting me at the Henry E. Rohlsen Airport.

How could I miss something so major like this in my life? Here I was, face to face with my sister. She told me that she tried to save me from my family, but she was afraid of getting sued. The laws in St. Kitts were very strict at that time. Mom would have been stoned and sent to jail for going out on her marriage and having a child for another man.

Through her, I learned that my three oldest siblings on my mom's side knew the truth about me. My oldest brother had witnessed Mom in the mountains having sex with my real father. Mom thought she was going through menopause when she conceived me. She had no idea she was pregnant.

My oldest sister, who was a police officer on the island, called her father and told him that he needed to be home because mom was here carrying someone else's child. Around the time I was conceived, my siblings' father had been doing different odd end jobs going to different islands for months at a time doing crop work. He would leave Mom with all the children and no money to feed them.

It seemed as though Mom had turned to another man for support and he, my real father, ended up taking on a married man's job. He fed all thirteen kids and made sure that they had money for school. When my oldest sister on my mom's side learned of her pregnancy, she and the other two eldest siblings decided to blackmail her.

I know Mom was afraid of them, but her pride was too high because she wanted people to think she had been pure all her life. She fell in love with my real father, and he did what any man would do—care for all of us. I just wanted to know how any child that came from a mother's womb would succumb to such evil. How could a child betray their own mother?

Denise argued with Mom, pleading her to see me. She had purchased school clothes for me, but Mom threw them in the garbage because she didn't want the truth to come out.

# CHAPTER SIXTY-TWO

Denise suggested that we should go to see our father's grave, and I agreed. When she took me to the cemetery, we walked in circles. She couldn't find his burial location. I didn't have much time before my departure flight. I was angry because his marker was made of two sticks and aluminum. Denise said that the hurricane must have blown away the marker.

I yelled, "When was the last time you visited Dad's grave?"

She looked at me, embarrassed, and said, "Only the day that they buried him."

A chill went through my body as I thought about the possibility that my dad did not have a proper burial. I wanted to leave and go home so I could think about how to make Dad happy and give him a proper tombstone so we could both have closure. I left shortly after because I did not want to hate my sister, and I needed space because it all became so overwhelming.

Denise ended up calling me almost every day trying to comfort me because she didn't know her sister had been abused by the man she thought was her father. She would sing little songs, telling me not to cry anymore. My sister was very careful about the information she shared because she didn't know how much I could handle. She also informed me that my mom actually knew she was pregnant and had planned to abort me because she had too many mouths to feed. It was our father that told Mom that he would take care of all her kids.

He wanted her to change my last names and give me to him so he could send me to my brother, his eldest son, so I could be cared for.

Mom had initially agreed but then changed her mind after giving birth to me.

# CHAPTER SIXTY-THREE

Denise and our brother, James, went against Mom's will and tried to help Dad with the deal he made with my mother. They wanted to make sure that she was ready to turn me over to his family. Mom threatened them with a lawyer so they took a step back because they didn't want any trouble.

My sister, Denise, told me that I was born before Mom's husband returned from his assignment. He was gone for at least a year, and I was already learning how to walk by then. My father was afraid for Mom because he didn't want her husband to come back and mistreat her and myself. Her husband came back angry knowing that the last child was not his, but he kept quiet about it. Denise had told Mom she couldn't hide me forever because the truth will eventually come out. Mom wanted Denise to be locked up because she felt she was being harassed.

# CHAPTER SIXTY-FOUR

The day after leaving St. Croix, I called the number Denise gave me. It was my brother, James. We talked for months, and we became very close. There was a point in my life when I had been laid off, and I didn't have any income and although James had not known me very well, he took my account number and began sending me money to help out until I got back on my feet.

There were times I didn't know how I was going to get by, and I would check my account to see a little surprise.

My daughter Chanelle received a new position that required her to relocate to Miami. I had asked James if he could help out and let her stay with him awhile and he agreed. The day that she moved in was the day that we met. I was so nervous to meet him for the first time, so I dragged my other daughter and her father for support. James was so inviting and although his place was small, he found space for us all. We crammed and slept on the floor, on the couch, his ab machine, and the bed! Culture style, as he would say.

When I finally saw him for the first time, I nearly lost my breath. His face was so familiar, and I instantly recognized him! His tall and slim stature, his large brown eyes, thin lips, and broad nose. He was my oldest brother's friend, the man that sat with me at my departure gate to New York at Miami International Airport when I was thirteen years old.

I tried to ask him questions about our father, but I couldn't get much out of him. He couldn't talk to me about our Dad because he appeared to have been mourning the death of his son, his partner as well as our father. He called his mother and sister over, and they sat with me and tried to answer all the questions that I had.

# CHAPTER SIXTY-FIVE

Through miscellaneous sources, I was told that my mother's husband had never held me, and since the very day that he saw me, they had slept in different bedrooms for the remainder of their marriage.

Cynthia, the same sister that was blackmailing Mom, got pregnant for a married man and left her child with Mom to raise. When she left for the States, she was pregnant once again, about three months. Shortly after her departure, she sent her wedding photos to show the new man in her life. She had this new guy convinced that her baby was his child. Denise revealed this to me and told me that the man that she was actually pregnant for was one of Denise's relatives.

Mom had also known about this, and they both had secrets on each other. It was part of the reason why Mom had remained silent. I wrote to Cynthia to let her know that I knew her secrets. I informed her that they, both her and Mom, were in the same boat and that no one was better than the other. I wanted her to stop blackmailing Mom, and in that moment, I was so proud to be a Palmer.

I learned that Dad had seven kids with another woman, and they were younger than me!

In all, I had a total of nineteen brothers and sisters from my parents that were still alive. I haven't been able to meet everyone just yet because I still fear rejection.

The village has remained silent about my mom, and I believe that she has a strong influence on them. I know Mom doesn't want the older generation to bring out the past. I never thought that by digging through the past that I would end up losing nearly my entire family on my mother's side.

Since the start of my journey, I have turned myself over to being more spiritual. I started meditating, I practice Buddhism, and I am learning how to be at peace with my inner self. I have learned so much in my life, especially working with adults that have autism. My experience with them has reopened old wounds because of the way society rejects these innocent souls. I know that it isn't our fault that people treat us differently because we are different. I know it is from the lack of understanding. I feel as though God has given me that chance to work with people with autism as an attempt to heal my soul as they are God's given children—angels—in my eyes.

There are times I cry myself to sleep out of frustration because I want to find a way to teach people how to accept and love people with autism. It hurts me because all they want is to be accepted, just as I had. It pains me to know that there are families that attempt to hide their relatives from the world. With that being said, I would end with a prayer for my deceased father as I know I will join him one day. My father died eight days after my birthday on March 28, 1994.

# CHAPTER SIXTY-SIX

Dear Dad,

It's your beloved daughter, Charmane. I am sorry you did not have the opportunity to get to know me and your grandchildren. I am so sorry for not knowing sooner about the truth about you being my father. I could have held you and told you how much I loved you. I wish Mom would have given me that chance to know you. Luckily for me, I have learned a lot about you still. I know how loving you were, and I know you would have never let your daughter suffer in this world. If you had a chance to be in my life, the world would have been a better place for us both. I have lost so much in my life. I lost you before I found you. I lived a life without a father, my dad. I know you tried to keep me from the pain, but I slipped through the cracks. I wanted to thank you for saving me because without you, Mom would have thrown me away.

In some ways, I didn't have either parent. I was alone. Some days, I feel that nothing could heal the bitterness I feel in my heart. I know you are listening to me. I hope that you can reach my heart and lay your hands on me so you could heal my pain. Please, Dad.

Your baby is home. I have been found, and I came a long way. I am coming to visit your grave to say goodbye and to personally tell you that I love you. I will never stop loving you. I will always keep you in my heart. Now that I know who you are, I remember when I was about twelve years old, and you were sitting in that chair. I am so sorry I didn't get to hold you then.

I have forgiven everyone who has hurt me, including my mother. I grew up strong and now, I live for you. Your kindness and your love shines through, and I promise you that I will continue to do so. I want everyone to know that we are good, caring, and loving people. I wish to be a good representation of you. Thank you for the gift of life, for bringing me into this world. I love you with everything that I have in me, and it feels so good to finally say the word "dad." I never thought I would have the chance to ever say the word. Rest your soul and be at peace because your daughter, Charmane Palmer, has been found.

Mrs. Perkins

I didn't know I was going to lose another mother. I thought I had many more years with her on this earth. We spent so much time together and when we weren't near one another, we were on the phone either talking or texting. She had a lot of free time, so we spoke often about everything about her life and mine. She was my angel, a friend, and a mother. She kept me strong during the hardest moments of my life, and I feel lost without her. I look over at my phone hoping that it will ring once more, and her name would light up. I wish the last text wasn't of her telling me that she was feeling ill. I wish that when she was told that she had cancer that she kept on fighting, but she didn't and died three days later. I guess she was tired of fighting. I hadn't realized that after all these years, I saw the soul of my mother inside Mrs. Perkins. She was the mother I could actually touch, hug, and embrace at any giving chance. When she left, I wish that it had been the soul of my birth mother so she could have some peace from all the madness, from all the drama in our familiar life. It hasn't been an easy process, but I hope that one day, I can actually move on. But watching that glow, her spirit leaving her helpless body was tough to swallow, and yet, I still smile and thank her for the thirty-plus years of being a mother to me.

My second mom whom I watched take her last breath in the hospital. She always called me Mother Theresa because she knew how pure my soul was. I could be broke and still find a way to make someone else happy. I would always find time to hear someone else's problem, and ignore my own. Having her for so long in my life, talking to her three times a day, and I was getting my healing. She never told her kids how much she loved them, but she told me how much she loved me and would always hang up the phone very quickly. Perk would never break down or let anyone know how much she loved them. After losing her to lung cancer, it made me think harder to reach out to my own mom. Letting her know that I could be next, or her, without a warning.

Perk never got her warning. She went in with a cold and died three days later. She hung on just for her kids and myself. I lost my best friend, Perk. But I gained unconditional love from her.

She had played a major part in my life. For thirty-one long years, she took on the role of being my mother and my dearest friend. We discussed the value and the meaning of family even though we didn't have the best family members to share that love we felt. After she took me in, she truly learned how evil my family was and did her best to show me what I should expect from people who actually loved me.

She was always concerned about her husband, and would update me on all the ways that he had hurt her. Cheating, lies, and deceit became her familiar. Every time she would find a random number in his wallet or pants pocket, she'd have me call the number on three way. Her heart was always aching, and I know each year she would pray for change.

She would ask for my opinion on her marital problems, and I would sit there and wonder, *Why me?* I wasn't mature enough to advise her on what to do with her forty-year marriage. My spirit was still childlike, unexperienced in the matter. I had to fight that inner child to stay within me so I could heal her soul and relieve her of her agony.

She was a woman of sacrifice. She hadn't worked for over twenty years because she chose to be a stay-at-home mother. She never had many friends that she could trust so she clung to me. She felt like I had all the right answers to whatever questions she asked because she was lost to the outside world, and I had to help bring her back to reality.

Perk couldn't talk to her own kids about her husband. They didn't know how verbally abusive he was to her. The way he would say mean things to her and humiliating her. I remember when she started losing weight, probably due to her undiagnosed cancer, and her husband asked her where her breasts had gone. It saddened me to hear that the man that she loved would say such a thing to her, so I bought her some sexy push up bras in all different colors to try to help her regain her confidence. She smiled at the gesture, and I could see in her eyes that she knew I would never judge her from her experiences.

Helping her was healing for me. I didn't care about being rejected once she had taken me in as one of her own. I finally had the strength not to care about what my blood relatives had to say about me because I had my mom, Perk, to comfort me.

# FINAL CHAPTER

After seeing the way life was lost in Mrs. Perk, I felt the urgency to see my own mother, so I decided to take a flight down to St. Kitts. The idea of losing a mother and going to see the one I've almost lost so many times made me grow anxious. I was nervous. I wanted to hug Mom and tell her all the things that have happened to me. I wanted to be consoled and told everything was going to be okay. I was fearful that this could be the last time I saw her. What if she suddenly grew ill and gave up the fight? What if she died with all her secrets after so many years of denial?

My thoughts were racing, but all I could do was wait. Upon my arrival, I grew weary. I was tired and my ear was giving me great pain. When I finally reached Mom's house, I was in unbearable pain. I ended up in the hospital the next day. I was told that I had a bad ear infection and was discharged. Strangely enough, as the days went by, I grew weaker. The look in my mom's eyes were full of fear and confusion. She wanted to know why I wasn't eating or getting any better. Seeing the pain in her eyes made me realize how much she loved me even if she didn't want to show me or my eldest daughter to see her compassion.

I knew St. Kitts didn't have the necessary equipment to help me get better so I had to force myself to get up and take the next available flight. Finally, three days later, I forced a smile and got up because I didn't want to die in my daughter's arm. I didn't want her to know how sick I really felt, but I knew I had to get back to the United States. When we touched down in New Jersey, we drove straight to the hospital, leaving our carry-ons in the back seat. Together, we learned that I had an inner and middle ear infection, pneumonia, and a mild heart attack all at once.

It was an eye-opener. I realized that after all these years, I had been so focused on helping others, and saving my mother from any obstacles that came her way. I was preoccupied raising my children, healing Luis, and shielding myself from evil attacks to even notice that my health was deteriorating. I spent eight days at the hospital and another week and a half away from work. I looked at both of my children and watched the scared look upon their faces; it made me realize I needed to change my life. I had to appreciate life more and give more to love my family and the man that I love that supported me, but I also needed to put myself first for once.

# ABOUT THE AUTHOR

Cecelia Ibarrondo was born and raised on the beautiful island of Saint Kitts. As a teenager, she immigrated to the United States in 1985 where she began her life in New Jersey. New Jersey continues to be her home. As the youngest of fourteen siblings, the mother of two (Charnelle and Simone), a friend, an employee, and a spouse, her life is a story waiting to be told and waiting to be read.

Cecelia cares about family, life, and learning. Her mission in life is to help the sick, the elderly, and the poor. Her debut book promises to move you to experience and release many emotions as she tells her life story.

She has such appreciation for life's experiences, which is evident in her book.

CPSIA information can be obtained
at www.ICGtesting.com
Printed in the USA
BVHW071123070119
537203BV00007B/864/P

9 781644 245750